"*Animal Bodies* is a ma[...]
ing, and grieving. Ro[...]
father, her dear frien[...], [...] complex force in her life.
Here, we read about rape, escape, affairs, and repair. There is wilderness and then, somehow, the clearing—both in her world travels and the dying around her. Thinking about death clarifies life, and Roberts knows the thin line between grief and joy, the importance of living fully and fighting for freedom without apology. This is hard-earned wisdom and liberation. I can't stop thinking about it."

—Lee Herrick, author of *Scar and Flower* and *Gardening Secrets of the Dead*

"I have been thinking about one particular Suzanne Roberts essay, 'Breaking the Codes,' since I first read it. Sometimes I open a closet door and my stomach drops, remembering one painful scene in her essay. Sometimes I see a group of teenagers and I wonder, and worry, about all of them. Roberts's writing rearranges me in some fundamental and necessary ways. A book like this, a book by her, is a book I desperately need."

—Camille T. Dungy, author of *Guidebook to Relative Strangers* and *Soil: The History of a Black Mother's Garden*

"Here, we travel with Roberts to beaches in Florida, to hospital rooms for chemotherapy, to Nashville honky-tonks, and to the Amazon rainforest. She carries to each of the locations her acute insight and her courageous and uncompromising desire to witness and record the world."

—Didi Jackson, author of *Moon Jar*

"These essays soar like falcons and dive octopus-deep; they carry the power and agility of tigers, the intelligent play of cetaceans. These essays are alive with lyricism and humor, thrumming with pain and pleasure and the complex spaces we inhabit between. Suzanne Roberts is a wonder and a force."

—Gayle Brandeis, author of *The Art of Misdiagnosis* and *Many Restless Concerns*

ANIMAL BODIES

animal bodies

ON DEATH, DESIRE, AND OTHER DIFFICULTIES

Suzanne Roberts

University of Nebraska Press | Lincoln

Acknowledgments for the use of previously
published material appear on pages 235–36, which
constitute an extension of the copyright page.

The University of Nebraska Press is part of a land-
grant institution with campuses and programs on the
past, present, and future homelands of the Pawnee,
Ponca, Otoe-Missouria, Omaha, Dakota, Lakota, Kaw,
Cheyenne, and Arapaho Peoples, as well as those of the
relocated Ho-Chunk, Sac and Fox, and Iowa Peoples.

Library of Congress Cataloging-in-Publication Data
Names: Roberts, Suzanne, 1970– author.
Title: Animal bodies: on death, desire, and
other difficulties / Suzanne Roberts.
Description: Lincoln: University
of Nebraska Press, [2022]
Identifiers: LCCN 2021036627
ISBN 9781496231024 (paperback)
ISBN 9781496231871 (epub)
ISBN 9781496231888 (pdf)
Subjects: LCSH: Roberts, Suzanne, 1970– | Authors,
American—21st century—Biography. | Loss
(Psychology) | BISAC: BIOGRAPHY & AUTOBIOGRAPHY
/ Personal Memoirs | BIOGRAPHY & AUTOBIOGRAPHY
/ Women | LCGFT: Autobiographies. | Essays.
Classification: LCC PS3618.O31628 Z46
2022 | DDC 814/.6 [B]—dc23
LC record available at https://lccn.loc.gov/2021036627

Set in Adobe Caslon Pro by Laura Buis.
Designed by L. Auten.

For my sisters,
Catherine and Cynthia

And for Kim and Ann Marie,
Camille and Kate,
Shoeleh, Christine, and Eve,
chosen sisters

Contents

Author's Note

This is a work of nonfiction, sourced from my journals and my own fallible memory, which is to say that while I have adhered to the truth of my own memories, others may have differing memories of the same events. Some names and distinguishing characteristics have been changed to protect the privacy of those involved.

ANIMAL BODIES

DEATH

And so it goes, and so it goes—
a woman knows what a woman knows.

> Words for losing places.
> *Hiraeth, saudade, morriña, dor.*
> The four chaise lounges of the apocalypse

    wait for us on the sands, knowing
time is a rope, a deck of cards, an empty glass—
        this place to sit by the ocean, watch
        sanderlings run from the waves,
            the long-fingered light of late afternoon.

Fear of disintegration
        hollows out my bones.
            I am becoming bird.

            —ILYSE KUSNETZ, from "Holding Albert Einstein's Hand"

The Essay Determines How It Will Begin

The essay is a transgression. The night you move back in with your ex-husband, you dream you are in bed with your mother.

The essay reveals the world we grew up in. Six days after Daddy's death, Mother goes on a date with the neighbor. When she comes home, she stands in the hallway, her naked breasts cupped in her hands, and asks, "Do you think I should have them lifted?"

The essay is a dilemma. When you leave Mother's house, you have a dream you abandoned a baby in the desert, forgot about her until it was too late. You write a poem about the dead baby, then climb on top of your ex-husband and imagine he's a dolphin. And you can breathe salt water.

The essay is unremarkable. When you think of Daddy, you remember his canvas shoes, rubber soled. Bought at the CVS. You think of him on his way to the grocery. Pushing a vacuum through the black end of his days.

The essay is a discovery. Found hidden in the filing cabinet: three bottles of rye, two fifths of gin, a carton of Winstons, between Daddy's files—plays he'd written, soap opera scripts, television treatments.

The essay is a bit of wobble in the system. Mother says you have wasted thousands on therapy; says she would have given you all the advice you needed for free.

The essay is a naming. You are forbidden to call her Mother. Mom is better. Mommy's best.

The essay is ruthless. Grandfather locked Mother in the dark coal house with the spiders. Set her on his lap every New Year's Eve and asked for a kiss. On the lips.

The essay is a reciprocity. Mother was a beauty queen. Nanny found her a man. Much older than young mother. And married.

The essay is a betrayal. Nanny made Mother drown a sack of kittens, cooked Mother's pet rabbit.

The essay is retribution. Nanny says it's only bad being blind in the middle of the night. When you are alone in the dark. When the black-haired girl there—she points in the direction of the ceiling—on the tightrope comes, asking for salt.

The essay is a dying wish. It's raining, and you are soaked from walking in it. Daddy has come out onto the wet streets in his car to find you. He begs you to get in, tells you he's dying. He makes you promise you won't break up with Mother. After he's gone.

The essay is a black hole. Into it went Daddy, his twin sister, and her kind husband. Young grandmother who burned up in a plane crash long before you were born. A grandfather and two more wives. The second wife drove into a snowplow on purpose after young uncle fell out the window. Three cousins in Auschwitz. Another cousin who liked the drink. A young brother-in-law who hoped eating from wooden spoons would cure cancer. An aunt who drowned in the bathtub on purpose. Your blind nanny, who could no longer make up her face for the pub. A dear friend who became your sister. Into the black hole went a guinea pig named Alfie, your two favorite dogs, and the fetus you carried briefly.

The essay is an accumulation of grief. Mother says to get over it.

The essay is a definition for love. You ask Daddy, "What's fuck?" Making love, he answers. You still don't understand. The boy from school said the kicked-in door was fucked. You try to equate that with love. You are seven, and you are afraid to ask more questions, that Daddy will shout at you, but he doesn't. Today he calls you kiddo, asks what kind of ice cream you would like on your cone. Mint chip, you say, I would like mint chip.

The essay is an inheritance. Mother keeps Daddy on the shelf. Says you better not throw them both away if she pops off. "When," you say, "when you pop off." Don't be mean, she says. Why are you always so mean?

The essay is a promise. You say you'll take them to the desert, watch the boxes burn, the smoke rising into a star-winking sky. You wouldn't dare, Mother says. And no water either. We'll be just fine in your closet.

The essay determines how it will end. A story is a papier-mâché carnation; the essay is a spotted purple orchid on your table. The one whose name you don't know. The one that looks fake but is real.

The Grief Scale

"I see we have a bin hog here."

"A what?" I asked, tugging my carry-on from the plane's overhead compartment.

"A bin hog." The woman stood behind me, waiting to deplane. I dropped my heavy roller bag onto the aisle and wished I had a clever comeback. Something smart and maybe a little bit mean. But I've always been too slow to deliver wit.

Instead I said, "That's a very unkind thing to say," and wheeled my bag to the Jetway. That's when my eyes went hot. My throat constricted, and the world fell under a shade of blur. There was no way I was going to let a bully in an ugly pink sweater set see me cry, so I picked up my overstuffed bag and rather than waiting in line for the escalator, I ran down the stairs.

Being called a bin hog would not normally make me cry. Not even if I was tired, like I was. I've been called a lot worse by both strangers and people I love. But I had come off a week of taking care of my very sick friend Ilyse, and suddenly there was everything—the tears and tightness of throat, the sadness simmering at the surface, the veil that had barely covered it all week finally slipping off.

During my layover in Houston, I stood in a corner near airport security, and I cried. I faced the oncoming passengers, who were busy putting their belts and shoes back on, stuffing their laptops into their cases. I wondered if a sobbing woman would be deemed a threat to airport security.

I later learned airports have an actual "cry room," though I don't think they call it that. My friend Kim made use of one on her way to a funeral. If you think about it, an airport cry room makes a lot of sense. During our most difficult moments, we usually pass through an airport—on our way to, or from, visiting a sick loved one. Or going to a funeral. Or coming home without a father.

I was in the Denver airport when I found out my father had died. He was sick, and I had missed my flight, so I was waiting for the next one to Los Angeles, hoping I would make it in time to see him but knowing—in that way you *know* but don't know—I hadn't. I called the hospital from the pay phone. This was before cell phones, or at least before I had one. I sat on my suitcase, the metal phone cord stretching the receiver down to my ear. I knew my father was sick because my stoic mother, who usually told me not to come home, finally said, "You'd better come now."

I was twenty-four and waitressing at a Mexican restaurant in Colorado, which helped support my life as a ski bum. It was spring break, so it was a busy night—an hour wait for a table—and it did not occur to me to leave work early. Not even if my father had been taken to the hospital in an ambulance.

After my shift, I drove home in a snowstorm and called the airline to book a flight. I packed a bag, and my boyfriend drove me to the airport. It did not occur to him to cancel the private ski lesson he was to teach the next day so he could go with me. "They're important clients," he had said.

At airport security, I was delayed because I had worn my overalls, a staple in my wardrobe at the time. If I wasn't wearing a waitress or ski school uniform, I was wearing baggy jean overalls, which now makes me wonder how I ever got a boyfriend. The overalls were decorated with metal buttons and latches, and when I went through the X-ray machine, I lit up like a Christmas tree. The woman called me over and scanned me with her angry, buzzing wand.

"It's my buttons," I said and started to cry. "I'm going to miss my flight."

"It's not my fault you're late. You should have planned better."

It did not occur to me to tell her my father was dying. That missing my flight would mean I wasn't going to be able to say goodbye. I stood there, red-faced, flushed hot with anger and with sadness, while her wand hovered over every metal button and clasp.

I ran to the gate, hauling my suitcase behind me, but they had shut the doors, and as everyone knows, once they shut that gate, the plane is as good as gone. Still, I begged. The woman behind the counter told me there was nothing she could do. That there would be another flight to Los Angeles and I could fly standby. She said she thought there might be a seat.

I walked to the pay phone to leave a message on my mother's answering machine. I wouldn't arrive until morning. I tried my sister, but she wasn't home either. I left messages on answering machines. I looked out the airport windows, watching the plane take off into a sky turning from black to purple, pink to pale blue. I went back to the pay phone and called the hospital. I was transferred twice. Each time I managed the words: "I'm calling for a patient, Paul Roberts."

The third transfer, the unfamiliar voice came on and asked, "Are you his other daughter?"

"Yes. How is he?"

"Where are you?"

"The airport. I missed my flight, but I board another one soon. I'll be there in a couple of hours. How is he?"

"Are you alone?"

"Yes." I didn't need to ask her how he was doing again. I knew. But the knowing also came with disbelief—the human mind can hold both at the same time; it's more complicated than denial—it isn't exactly a rejection of knowledge but the mind's ability to hold opposing ideas at the very same time.

My mouth seemed to move, words coming out without any real connection to me. I felt outside of myself, watching from somewhere else. "He died, didn't he?" I said, my voice a squeak. I wanted to say the words so she didn't have to. To make it easier on this stranger, this person who had possibly attended to my father's dying.

The voice on the phone said, "I'm so sorry. Are you okay? Is there anyone there with you?"

"I'm fine. I'm okay." But I was in full cry. The gate agent who had told me I hadn't made it onto the last plane looked over at me from behind her desk. Everyone else was trying not to stare at me, keeping extra busy, which made me feel better and worse all at the same time.

"Tell my sister I know," I said. "That way when she picks me up, she doesn't have to tell me. So she doesn't worry about telling me. Tell them all I know."

"Are you sure you're okay?"

The gate agent announced the plane was boarding. "I have to go," I managed to say and hung up. I sobbed as quietly as possible, waiting for my group to be called.

The woman at the counter waved me over. "I noticed you may have gotten some bad news."

I nodded.

"Your boarding pass?" she asked.

I handed it to her.

She looked at it, ripped it up, and handed me another one.

"This seat's in the back, but there's no one next to you."

"Is it a window?" Because I'm afraid of flying, I need to stare at the wing if the plane encounters turbulence, as if my gaze will hold the plane in the air. This has been my flying ritual for as long as I remember, needing to control the uncontrollable. But if my father really had died, which I still wasn't sure I believed, would the universe really kill us both in one day? Regardless of the laws of separate probabilities and chance, I concluded this was not possible—my own strange and private logic that sometimes helps, sometimes doesn't.

"It's a window."

"Thanks," I managed. I couldn't think too much about this kindness because sometimes it's the kindness that makes you cry, even more than the nastiness. Or maybe it's the juxtaposition of the two.

Lining up, finding my seat, and putting my bag in the overhead bin came as a relief. I had something to do. And I knew when each action was complete. As the gate agent promised, the middle seat remained unoccupied. I leaned toward the window and watched the mountains of Colorado recede, the glaring blue winter sky, the wavering silver airplane wing.

This was back when the airlines provided meals, even on a two-hour flight. The flight attendant offered me breakfast, but I waved it away.

"I'll have yours," the woman in the aisle seat said, so I accepted the food and then handed it over.

"Are you sick, honey?" she asked.

"No," I said, "just sad." She nodded, and then she made quick work of her two meals. Usually, I feel like I have to explain myself to anyone who asks, strangers included, but I couldn't do it, so I left it at that and went back to wing watching. I tried to picture my father's spirit, floating among the wispy clouds, but I couldn't do it. I couldn't see him as a ghost any more than I could imagine him dead. And then wild thoughts formed. Maybe someone had made a mistake! It's been known to happen in hospitals. Maybe it wasn't my father who died but some other man! It couldn't be true I would never see my father again. My mind would not concede this was possible.

All life leads to death, so why is it impossible to imagine? The world is made up of the things we know. How can we go on without all of them arranged around us? Sometimes we can't, but we must.

The plane landed, and I walked toward the exit, hoping my sister had gotten the message.

Cindy was standing with her boyfriend, and they were both wearing black sunglasses. I said, "I already know. You don't have to tell me." Cindy hugged me.

We loaded into my sister's baby-blue convertible Mustang and headed for the 405. The Southern California sunshine glimmered off the oil-streaked freeway. It was 9:00 a.m. and already eighty degrees. I took off my jacket and sweater. We rode with the top down, and my hair struggled against the wind. We looked like a family on our way to a picnic or the beach. Like everything was fine. The line between joy and grief incidental.

One death. We never quite get used to it.

In my memory Cindy and I didn't talk to each other on the car ride home. When Cindy and her boyfriend dropped me off, I walked into the dark house, where my mother and my oldest sister, Cathy, were trying to sleep. My childhood bedroom was free, so I lay on my bed, and I stared at the popcorn ceiling. I remember thinking it reminded me of sea-foam. I felt tired but couldn't sleep. I could hear the pounding of my heart in my ear, so I turned onto my side and put my ear on the edge of the pillow, a trick my father had taught me. Daddy used to say some are too heart aware, but if you lie on your right side with the pillow at the edge of your ear, you won't hear the incessant beating.

I felt curious about the details of my father's death but didn't have the courage to ask. I felt the creep of guilt for not being there, a shadow that would stay over me for the rest of my life. Or at least until now, more than twenty years later.

I would lie in my childhood bed until I heard the rest of my family rustle. Then we looked through the house for a letter. Though Daddy didn't kill himself, he knew he was dying, and I was sure he left some sort of message for us—his three daughters. Something that would make us feel better. I searched drawers, filing cabinets, cupboards. I came back with a couple of bottles of whiskey and a carton of cigarettes, his hidden contraband.

Later I found out my sisters had already stumbled across another stash of his hooch, and when they got back from the hospital early that morning, they poured themselves a shot and drank to Daddy. I wished I had been there. I was glad I wasn't. I couldn't decide. I still can't.

My mother told me Daddy had hung on, but they were all telling him to go. Then she told him I had arrived, that I was there, and he died. "He was waiting for you," she said. "He wouldn't die until you got there." She said this as if it would make me feel better. This lie. This cruelty. This kindness.

"But I didn't get there. Why did you tell him I was there?"

"Suzanne, you don't know how hard it was to see him like that. You would understand if you had been there."

"But I wasn't."

"You're missing the point, I think. You're just tired." Whenever I said or did or felt differently than my mother would have liked, she made an excuse for me: you're sick, you're upset, you're tired, you're drunk, you've misunderstood, you're just in a bad mood.

I wasn't there, and he must have known it, didn't he? The wild thoughts take over: if she hadn't told him, would he have still been alive in the morning when I got there?

And if I had been there, maybe I wouldn't dream him alive only to watch him die. In my dreams I find out my father has been alive all these years; my mother, as it turns out, had been lying to me. But by the time I realize he isn't dead, it's too late. He is dying. Rather than see him die once, I have seen him die countless times.

I hadn't meant to write about my father. I sat down intending to write about my sick friend Ilyse and how hard that was, being there with her but not being able to make any difference in whether she would get better or not. About taking her to the doctor in the sprawling Florida cancer hospital. And how when I left her and landed at the Houston airport, I lost my shit because of everyday cruelties. I wanted this to be about how we should always be kind because the person we are unkind to might have spent a week sleeping on a couch with two cats she is allergic to, waking up to clean out their litter boxes; she might have sat next to her sick friend in the slanted light of the rainy afternoons, watching her sleep. She might be worn thin by hope.

It's easier to accept grief for the dead than grief for the dying, so we try not to think about it; instead, we enter the land of the absurd, and we deny where we're all inevitably headed—into the terrifying unknown. To try to make sense of it all, we put our grief on another kind of scale—one that will measure its weight. Maybe this is so we can one-up each other in the game of our own unhappiness.

The workplace measures grief by days off. I can take three days off for a parent or spouse. Two days for a grandparent but only if I have to travel. I took the days off for my British grandmother. I figured she would want me to even if it wasn't enough time to get to England and back. But our emotional attachments cannot be quantified by how direct our bloodlines are to those who have died. I have known people who have said losing a dog was worse than losing their mother. When my favorite dog, Riva, died, I wailed into the furry cuff of her neck, collapsed on the floor of my kitchen. Even still, it was nothing like losing a father, at least not for me. But even my dog's death brought me back again to my father, that familiar pool, dark and deep.

Grief is like water—all water is wet; all grief is difficult. Though it's one thing to wade into a small pool of grief, another thing entirely to drown in its sea. But water is water, and each drop adds up to become an ocean, even if it begins with a single tear.

I have a friend who says grief used to be one room in the house. After she and her husband lost their son, grief was the only room.

I cannot access grief without metaphor, a way to measure the unmeasurable. The ways we recognize a musical score—by its scales, the repeating octaves—is similar to the way we recall grief. A musical scale can transport us to another time and place, as if the music has always lived inside us, and like the notes that bring music out of our bodies, one grief recalls another. Each new sadness dips into the well of the rest, carrying the old grief with the new.

You'd think we would have gotten used to it by now—this living and dying—but we haven't.

I'd meant to say something about kindness, too, and its opposite, which is more heartlessness than meanness. But maybe that's its connection to the all-too-full-of-heart grief. Without love there is no grief.

After I returned home, Ilyse soon went into remission, and we laughed about the Bin Hog Lady from the airplane, thinking up witty comebacks—Ilyse is better at this than I am: "I guess pigs really do fly!" or, "At least I'm just a bin hog, whereas you're a hog," or, "Lady, you've just become a character in my next story."

But the remission is over now, and we're back to hanging our hearts on hope. We can hear the scales of that old song playing again. The music never really disappeared—even when we refused to listen—and now it's back.

They say, "That's life!" and whoever they are turns out to be right.

I'd also meant to talk about the man with the hole in his throat and the shining heads of beautiful young women and the piano that played itself in the lobby of the Florida hospital. And the crude crimson scrawl through the word CANCER on the kind doctor's name tag—like a child's red crayon crossing out a mistake. And the pharmacy with the row of IV bags hanging from the ceiling like a plastic chandelier. I had meant to write the new yet horrifying words now in my lexicon: PET scans and ports, lesions and bone strengtheners, flare responses and fentanyl lollipops.

And I had meant to say something about the green smell of rain and the blue herons walking along the marsh on their elegant legs. And something about how the gray sky fell onto the windshield of the car and the way the wipers pushed the water away, the window clearing just long enough to make out the highway before us.

The Grief Scale   15

Eight Hours

1.

I let Brandon ski in the front of the line all day, and I helped him up every time he fell down. He ate as many Tater Tots at lunch as he wanted. He ate cake until he felt sick. I couldn't eat. I made sure he found the most "gold nuggets" at the gold mine, and he got to ski through the bear cave first. I told the other children in the class it was because it was Brandon's birthday. That part was true, but that wasn't why I was being so nice to him.

2.

On our way to the chairlift, my supervisor pulled me aside. "Brandon's father hit an aspen tree on his first run of the day. His aorta detached. He was dead by the time patrol got there." The family decided to let Brandon finish ski school, enjoy his sixth birthday, before finding out. Before the world changed. "Make sure that little boy has fun. Do you understand what I'm saying?" my supervisor asked. I assured her I did. My own family kept secrets; I could do this.

"Let me carry your skis, Brandon." My voice cracking on its own.

"Carry mine."

"Me too. And mine."

"It isn't your birthday," said the pit in the throat. "It's only Brandon's birthday."

3.

The aspen tree is part of a clonal colony derived from a parent tree. Each clone lives above ground for up to 150 years. The root system can live underground thousands of years. The aspen on the edge of the intermediate run still adds to its rings. New clones emerge from the earth. The man who hit the tree has been gone for twenty years. Brandon is now a grown man, and every birthday is the anniversary of his father's death. The aspen tree will be there after even he's gone.

4.

"I want to ski in front."

"Well, I want a million dollars."

"But, why can't I ski in front?"

"You can ski second behind Brandon."

"Why does Brandon get to ski in front the *whole* time?"

"It's his birthday."

"It was my birthday last week. And I want to go through the bear cave first."

"It isn't your birthday *today*. It's only Brandon's birthday today. Let's sing to him while we ski."

5.

Brandon was the last one to be picked up. We always referred to the stragglers as "the least loved children," their parents drinking toddies at the bar. But I didn't even think it. Instead, I let him choose a video and sat with him as he laughed at the animated figures.

6.

The mother finally came in with the ski patrol. "Mommy," he called. She hugged him. Her face scrunched up in a red and swollen way. Gravity had changed everything.

7.

The bark of an aspen is white and soft and strong.

8.

"You can't cry," my supervisor had said. "You have to make sure that little boy has a good time." Good time, good time, good time. The not-knowing-yet day. Happy birthday, dear Brandon, happy birthday to you. We sing, and we ski. We are airplanes, and then we are race cars. We play, and we play at pretending.

The Same Story

In this story two young women are pregnant at the same time by the same man. One of the women is a musician and a writer and a feminist, and she sports tattoos and body piercings before they are cool. The other woman is an outdoorsy graduate student and a feminist, and she wears J.Crew sweater sets and Mary Janes. The musician calls the graduate student "Miss Goody Two-Shoes." The graduate student calls the musician "The Slut." I am one of these women, or was, and now I realize it doesn't matter which one. What matters is the man is let entirely off the hook by two young women who call themselves feminists.

Though both the musician and the graduate student could tell you stories, I can tell only mine: I was twenty-four, and my father had recently died. Daddy worked hard at being a writer and a drinker but was successful only in the drinking. He shouted at me when he drank, but he was Daddy, so I loved him. I was just starting to be adult enough to reconcile the complicated feelings I had for my father, but he died before I realized his drinking did not mean he didn't love me. He died feeling like he had failed me. And that has always made me feel that really it was I who failed him.

I met the man, an artist and a writer and a drinker, three months after my father's death. The way things happened to that twenty-four-year-old now seems very clear. For six months I studied life drawing with him at the community art center and swapped stories and poems with him. He was almost ten years older than me. I drank with him, and I slept with him when he wanted me to. Frequently, we shouted at each other. I broke up with him when he told me to fuck off or asked me things like "Who do you think you are? Do you think you're special?" I wasn't sure who I was entirely, and even though I had grown accustomed to my father's shouting, I had a small idea that perhaps I was someone who didn't deserve to be yelled at. But then again, I wasn't sure about anything, so we'd soon get back together and start the whole mess of a thing again.

My friend Andy referred to the artist-writer-drinker as my on-again, off-again. One night that November, my on-again, off-again came to my house. Technically, we were off and not on, but my housemates were on a road trip, so I would not have to feel embarrassed over Cheerios the next day, admitting I had let my on-again, off-again back into my bed. So I let him in, and I let him fuck me. I let him fuck me with no condom, only spermicide, even though I had an idea he was also fucking another girl and even though he had once called me by her name right after sex and then said he meant his cat, who conveniently shared her name.

You know what's coming next. In retrospect nothing is a surprise.

The word *mistake* comes from the fourteenth-century Old Norse *mistaka*, meaning "to wrongly take," as in "to take the wrong course of action." More recently, the word *mistake* has also come to mean, specifically, "unintended pregnancy."

I went to the clinic, and after a simple urine test, they called and confirmed it. I listened to the nurse telling me to avoid caffeine and alcohol. I put the phone back on the hook, then picked it back up, called my friends Judy and Ben, and asked if they wanted to drink beers with me at the beach. We sat at Montaña de Oro, watching the sunset with giant cans of Foster's. I didn't tell them why I had called. Judy and Ben, my embryo and I—we watched the sun sink below the Pacific and talked of other things, things I do not remember. I came home, now full of forty ounces of Foster's courage, picked up the phone, and called my on-again, off-again. He wasn't home, was maybe out somewhere with his other girl. I knew he would not call me back unless I said this: "On-again, off-again, it's me. Please call me back. I'm—I'm pregnant."

He called back the next day, and when I answered the phone, he said, "Hey, Mama." He said this as if it was cute or funny. Yet twenty-four-year-old me thought I needed him. In truth I thought it worse to be pregnant by someone who wasn't my boyfriend, even if I would never tell anyone about it. What a slut! I hated how that word sounded. How it felt. In the end language turned out to be everything. I went back to my on-again, off-again because of the word *slut*—a repulsive word, a word I hated but nevertheless applied to myself.

My on-again, off-again and I didn't ever talk about it, but somehow there was a nonverbal agreement we'd be back on again, at least for a while. And so we were.

One afternoon a few days after I'd found out, we lay on the futon in his loft, and I watched dust float in and out of the yellow slant of winter light. I counted the dead moths on the windowsill. My on-again, off-again was tired, maybe from too much Bushmills, and he snored into my hair. His hand rested on my stomach, and I thought, "We are three, not two. I am two, not one." I can't remember whether I had already made the appointment, but I had made up my mind. Even though I pictured a floating, fishlike life inside of me, I needed to protect my future, one I had only begun to allow myself to imagine in a hazy dreamworld sort of way.

I wanted to know what my on-again, off-again was thinking. Maybe he, too, did math equations in his head—three not two, forty-two and fifty-one at a high school graduation. I didn't ask. At one point he said, "The child would be good-looking, artistic, and smart." This made things worse for me because it was likely true. I didn't ask my on-again, off-again if he wanted to keep the baby, and he never said anything. Another unspoken agreement: it was my decision to make, and for that I am still grateful. But that doesn't mean it was easy.

Here is what I wrote in my journal on December 3, 1994: *I am so upset. I miss Daddy. Is life really this hard? I am unloved. I am killing my baby. I am two. I sit here as two. I hurt and I cry and this page is getting blurry. Enough of this. Enough.*

At the time I did not know his other girl was pregnant too. Would that have made me feel worse? Or better? I have no way of knowing.

For many years I tried very hard not to think about all of this, but as I bring it back to the surface of my skin, I remember something else, a thing I didn't dwell on at the time, but now I see it connects everything: the other woman had recently lost her mother. When a parent dies, no matter what age you are, there's that *I'm next* feeling. When you are young, and maybe even when you are old, that realization can bring with it a recklessness, a disregard for the self. For me that meant searching out a chaos, as if that was the only thing that could fill my chest's black hole. Of course, it only made matters worse, widened the gap. There was no way to fix the problem—my father was dead, and there was nothing I could do to bring him back.

The first time I met my on-again, off-again, he made a comment about the leather attaché case I was carrying, and I told him it had been my father's. Then I added, "My father just died."

"When?" he asked.

"In March."

"This past March?"

"Uh-huh."

"I'm really sorry."

"It's okay," I said. "We're all going to die someday."

"Wow," he said.

"What?"

"It's just that . . . that's very existential."

"I guess," I said, not really sure what that had to do with my father's death or me, but I was reading Camus and Sartre and Simone de Beauvoir, so I took it as a compliment. As an understanding of something—of what I'm still not sure.

In those months after my father died, I couldn't seem to stop crying. Every time I waited at a traffic light with three distraction-free seconds on my hands, I wept uncontrollably. I didn't want to cry all the time, so I tried not to think about my father or myself; the casual affair with my on-again, off-again was a good distraction.

After I found out I was pregnant, I tried to run it away. I woke up in the morning, downing coffee and skipping break-fast, and I ran more miles than ever before. Three, seven, thir-teen miles. I jogged down to the beach, splashing through the foaming sea; I struggled up sand dunes and back down them; I let the rain snap at my face like rubber bands; and I shivered in the salty fog. I didn't see this as punishment at the time. I just hoped to come home, see a petal of blood on my panties. Something in me felt broken, unfixable.

Mistaka, in the Old Norse, also means "to miscarry." But no matter how many miles I logged, I couldn't run the pregnancy away.

My current self would not call a fetus "a baby" and would never refer to terminating a pregnancy as "killing a baby." But at twenty-four, and pregnant, I did. I wanted to really feel it. I felt it was important to know exactly what I was about to do and still make the decision I needed to make, as if looking at one kind of horror straight on would diminish the other. I was hurting already and wanted to hurt more, as if this newer hurt could rub out the old, deep hurt.

The night before the abortion, I agreed to go to a holiday party with my on-again, off-again. In truth I knew if I used the party as a test, passive-aggressively hoping he would stay home with me rather than attend the party, he would fail, and that would mean I had failed too. And I had already failed enough.

The hosts were two lovely gay men, Raphael and Simon. They had created a Barbie nativity scene for the party, featuring a Black Barbie, Cher Barbie, and Aladdin—"a much sexier alternative to that eunuch Ken," Raphael declared. "How about a Bellini, Sweetheart?"

Vanessa, a pug in a sequined gold tutu, mingled with the party guests, wheezing and barking every time the doorbell chimed. Raphael showed me a picture of himself in drag. He said, "But don't think I want to be a woman, Sweetheart. I like my dick so much that what I want is another one. Another Bellini?" Normally, a tutu-clad pug named Vanessa, a drag queen glamour shot, a multicultural Barbie nativity scene, and free-flowing champagne would cheer me up considerably. Instead, I sucked down one drink after another and thought, *I'm pregnant, I'm pregnant, I'm pregnant.* I spent most of the evening with Vanessa, wondering if anyone could tell that the drunk girl petting the pug was pregnant.

If this were fiction, I could not tell you that on the day of the abortion, the clouds rumbled in, pleat after gray pleat, the sky coughed with thunder, dead leaves circled in wind funnels. Or that lightning cracked open the sky. It would be too obvious, heavy-handed. But it is true; the rain indeed fell in sheets. Lightning divided a gray sky. I told my on-again, off-again I wanted to walk to the clinic, three blocks from his house.

"It will take three minutes," I said. "We'll bring an umbrella. I will be fine!"

We walked along the rain-soaked pavement, the wind shaking waxy magnolia leaves onto the sidewalks. The gray-green clouds climbed the sky. The passing motorists wondered, perhaps, what those two were doing out there on such a day, huddled under a shared umbrella in the pouring rain.

We arrived at the Planned Parenthood clinic. I told my on-again, off-again he did not have to come into the abortion room with me. "It's bad enough I have to be there," I said, hoping to lift the mood—another attempt to let him off, to protect him. I didn't know that within a few weeks he would sit in that same waiting room again, maybe even be there with her for the procedure. I didn't want to know, and I never asked.

He would tell me it wasn't his. The other boyfriend had allegedly gotten her pregnant, and my on-again, off-again was merely being a good friend. Though the supportive friend role didn't really fit the character of my on-again, off-again, I chose to believe him. Why? Maybe because I wanted to deny I was one of the points on an ugly triangle. Even now, my mind drifts to the thought: *Maybe he really was telling the truth?* I cannot help but carry the sensibilities of that twenty-four-year-old girl inside my middle-aged self, even though, deep down, we both know better.

At the clinic I peed in a cup to make sure. I hoped it had gone away, but it hadn't, despite the many miles I had run, the many cups of coffee and glasses of wine I had downed. I filled out the paperwork, lying about the date of my last period. I wasn't technically far enough along for the procedure, but I figured a couple of days wouldn't make a difference. Better to do it early, I thought. The earlier, the better—the smallest version possible of the not-yet-living.

I took the little blue Valium with water from a Dixie cup and then waited next to a blonde teenager, who wore pigtails and was crying, and I remember feeling angry with her, wanting to turn to her and spit out my mother's favorite three-word phrase: *Get over it.* I see now my anger was not for her but for me, and I have wished I could reach back through the years and say "I'm sorry" to us both. The only way to do this, I now see, is in the telling.

Above me there was a poster of Tom Selleck, mustachioed and suntanned, leaning out of a red Ferrari. Another poster featured a basket of kittens, a ball of yarn. Some inspirational script looped across the poster, but I can't remember what— something about friendship. Not only have I not spoken about this day; I have never written about it except once, years later, obliquely in a poem. Even in the journal I obsessively kept then, I mentioned the abortion only once. Too private, I must have thought, even for the page.

But still, I remember the posters and the rain and the walk to the clinic. And the doctor, who was built like a fireplug and wore her brown hair cropped short. I remember the thin membrane of tissue between me and the metal table. And the nurse who held my hand, told me everything would be all right. She was right; it was. And it wasn't. Lightning zippered across the sky, and the lights flickered off and on. And so did the abortion machine. Over the starting and stopping vacuum noise, the doctor said, "Are you sure about the date of your last period? I can't find it. It's too small." And I thought, *Find it, find it, find it.* I prayed to the electricity spirits, *Stay on, stay on, stay on.* Then the lights would flicker, and the humming-sucking sound would stop.

Start. Stop. Start.

Stop.

"I got it. But it's so small, I'm not sure I got it all," the doctor finally said. I squeezed on the nurse's hand, and I thank the world for providing people like her to people like twenty-four-year-old me.

Then the face of my on-again, off-again appeared over me like some sort of long-haired, bespectacled god. The Valium had finally kicked in, and I wondered, "Who let him in?" According to the nurse, though, I had asked for him.

"How are you doing?" he asked.

"Well?" It came out more like a question than an answer.

"Was it terrible?" he whispered.

"Terrible enough."

"I'm sorry," he said.

"Me too. I'm fine. Don't worry."

We walked home in the rain. The fallen magnolia leaves were purplish green splotches, like wet bruises on the sidewalk. The streets, rainbow puddled, smelled of water and oil. We didn't tell the nurses about the walking. Surely, they would not have allowed it. But I was fine! I asked my on-again, off-again to drive me to the post office. I wanted to check my post office box for poetry rejections. For some reason he complied. I don't remember the ride to the post office, the tires on wet pavement, the rain-filled gutters, the steam rising from the pavement. I don't remember hitting the shiny post office floor. I remember only the crowd around me and begging my on-again, off-again to get me out of there before the paramedics, who were already on their way, arrived. He managed that, against all of the onlookers' good advice.

I wasn't about to get pregnant again. I didn't have health insurance back then, but because of the abortion, I had learned about Planned Parenthood and was able to get a prescription for the pill. I walked through a group of people carrying posters decorated with dead babies. I remember thinking about the irony of this because they had not been at the clinic on that rainy day in December. I remember wanting to say something to them, to tell them I'd already killed my baby, but then I realized their fun is in getting people riled up, so I did my best to ignore them. The pills wrecked my mood and left me potbellied and pock faced, but I never got pregnant again.

My on-again, off-again kept fucking the other girl, and by March I could no longer delude myself, so I confronted him. That's when I learned she had had an abortion at the same clinic, the same month. And then I did a very bad thing: I called her names. I did not think her pain might have matched my own, that her mistakes were my own. That we were not only part of the same story—we were the same story. Looking back, I see we should have been on one side, with on-again, off-again on the other. We were more similar than different in the things that mattered. We might have consoled each other; none of my friends had lost parents yet, and no one wanted to talk about death. But we were divided by words and by the self-hatred we'd learned to adopt as girls, as young women. Language and thought are inextricably bound. If we allow our language to disintegrate, so goes our thinking. We are reduced to sound bites and stereotypes, to The Slut and Miss Goody Two-Shoes.

I finally wrote my on-again, off-again a letter, in which I spun all the meanness from my scarred body into words, and sent it to him, finally ending things for good. I hurt him deeply, and for years I felt guilt over that because in many ways he, too, was a broken person. Now the guilt is for the way I regarded both my twenty-four-year-old self and his other woman.

According to my doctor, my chance of getting pregnant now is less than 1 percent. Just being middle-aged me is more reliable than the pill. "Never been pregnant," I've told every gynecologist I've gone to in the past twenty years, as if saying it makes it so. And I suppose saying that has helped me to forget, but more than forgetting, what I've really done is to allow my shame to cultivate callousness. A fourteenth-century Scandinavian source reports that *mistake* means "to misinterpret," and for all these years I have done just that. For years I chose to believe the other woman's abortion had nothing to do with me, which has made me a poor excuse for a feminist.

I don't regret the decision I made, though I do regret having to make it in the first place. I also regret my two-decade subscription to guilt and blame. And sometimes I catch myself doing the math: kindergarten, sweet sixteen, graduation—all the usual markers for the almost person. It has taken me a long time, but I've realized I can live with this sort of longing while letting go of the shame.

As it turns out, language still turns out to be everything—in this story two young women are pregnant at the same time by the same man. In this story neither woman is to blame.

Becoming Bird

In Memory of Ilyse Kusnetz (1966–2016)

The Steller's Jay

The message from your husband, Brian, reads: *This morning. I can't write it. There are no words.* And also this: *I am fucking broken inside.*

I walk out onto the deck to look for flying things. A jay shrieks from a lodgepole pine. Fucking bird, I think. Obnoxious noisy Steller's jay.

I leash the dog and run the trail toward the creek. A hawk arcs over our heads. The red tail catches the sun as the bird enters the sky.

Later I mention the hawk to my friend Kim, and she brings me a book about birds. The book sits on top of a pile of other books. I want to continue believing in nothing.

The Raven

The next morning I turn on my phone, and there is a poem from you. *That's nice*, I think. I read it, then try to close the page, but it won't close. I keep trying and wonder if phones can get viruses, if that's why my phone is frozen. I turn it off and back on. The poem is still there. I read it again. Nothing.

I say to you, "Hello, Ilyse, my dear poet friend." I hit the boxed *x*, and the window closes.

Brian sends me a manuscript of your new work, the poems you wrote when you were dying. In it you warn, "I will be your sweet poltergeist." I laugh because I am glad and because I believe we must be laughing together.

A raven lands on the branch of a Jeffrey pine. Its feathers and beak, inky as a night without stars. I try to take a photograph, but the dog barks it away.

The Red-Tailed Hawk

Very soon it is my birthday, and I go out onto the deck to straighten up the patio furniture for a party. A hawk circles above, soaring with its wings at a slight dihedral. It's October, I tell myself, autumn: the season of the hawk.

I finally read the book my friend Kim brought me on hawks. *Buteo jamaicensis.* The red-tailed hawk's adaptations include color vision, sharp talons, hollow bones. I remember you telling me the cancer was eating you from the inside out, hollowing your bones.

You said the cancer adapted, created a cloak of invisibility, a clever bastard. I learn hawks are as fierce as they are beautiful, and they have scales on their legs so they can rip the heads from venomous snakes without danger. I wonder about that—what that would look like.

That afternoon I leash the dog and take off running down the trail. I run a few miles and then turn back toward home, and a red-tailed hawk flies above my head, carrying something like a whip.

Still alive, it flings itself against gravity.

I stop, and the dog sniffs at the trail, and I fear I'm seeing imaginary things. But I'm not. It is a hawk and a snake, and the world behind the world comes at me from behind my eyes. I stand on the trail, between the manzanita and the pine, and I weep.

I know what it seems like—it seems that way to me too. But I would not tell this story if it wasn't true.

The Northern Gannet

I arrange for your friends, all poets, to travel to Florida to see you. We walk the beach, come across a dead northern gannet: a seabird that can dive more than a hundred feet, plunging into the ocean. It had likely flown off course. At least that's what the biologist said. It was perfect, the neck curved like an elegant question. The other poets take photographs. Snow white on the sand.

We come to your home in Orlando. Your hair is now cut short and an orangey color, patchy with the scalp showing through. You say the pain stems from your knees. You show us the radiation mask.

"No one saw this coming," you say.

"I can't be an invalid," you say.

I can see the dying flame in you and wonder if anyone else notices. We talk about the unlikely Republican candidate, and your candle flickers, and I see it: the dying of the light. Sometimes the world comes to us in cliché.

We hold hands tightly while another of our poet friends recites Attar; she says the divine is an ocean and we are all moving toward it.

And then the rain comes, a deluge. And you say, meaning the rain, "It's nice, right?" And we all agree that it is.

You say when you married just five years ago, you did not think it would come to this. This was not *supposed* to happen. I hold your hand and try not to show the sadness. Try not to show how thin the hope has worn.

Later we eat off plates your mother made. It is only this simple and easy act that makes sense.

And you tell us you planted an orange tree. You say the flowers will bring the bees; you hope they will bring the bees. We all say we hope so too.

When we leave, I tell Brian we will do this again, all of us coming, and he agrees and I agree, but the light has left his eyes, too, and we are agreeing to things we no longer believe.

The Gull

You finally make it to the ocean, and when you look up at the sky, you shake your fist and say, "Fuck you, God."

You tell me you wanted to keep the cancer from taking a toe-hold, that you have seen how it can go and it isn't good.

You walk into the ocean, bend to the water, and let the foam curl around your fingers. You bring the salty, fetid decay of life to your face. You breathe in. We all breathe in. We bring your chair to the edge, and the ocean surges around you. You lift your feet, and you laugh.

"Who gets brain tumors?" You ask me, the ocean, God.

The only answer is *You do. You did.* But I just shake my head while the ocean rumbles and God stays silent.

A fisherman catches a gull on his line. The bird is frantic, swooping with jerky motions, straining against the line. Another gull flies nearby, screaming. The man tries to catch the trapped gull, and I watch as if my life depends on it.

Another one of our poets helps him, and the man catches the gull, untangles her, and lets her go. And when the bird enters the sky, something giant and sad lets go in me too.

You ask us about our words, our poems, our work. And you say, "When life gives you shit . . ."

"Make a shit sandwich?" I ask.

"Yes, with ketchup," you say, and we laugh.

And then you say, "I wasn't expecting this. It wasn't supposed to happen this way."

The Sanderlings

This time I have come to see you on my own. We are at the beach again and watch sanderlings chase the retreating sea, dig for sand crabs, then run back onto shore again on swift legs. We giggle because there is something so funny about these little birds and their flickering legs and because the sunlight reminds us of girlhood and the long days of summer when friends become sisters.

We walk through the curtain of sea-foam, looking for shells. The usual topics of conversation—upcoming projects, travel, summer plans—no longer hold us. There is only this, and I realize I have never been so present in my life. I want to tell you this, but I don't because you already know.

I pick up a large shell with many smaller shells attached to it: a treasure. When I hand it to you and tell you to keep it, you cup it in your hands, turn it over, and say, "Are you sure? It's so special."

I hadn't intended this to be the last time. Only searching the shore for interesting rocks and shells and shading our eyes from the light.

The night before I fly home, you say, "You are my sister," and I answer, "Yes." But you say in a very serious tone, "No. Really." And you do a thing with the nest of your palm against your heart, and then you kiss your hand and put it back to your chest, and I say, "Yes, I know," because I do.

I close the door of the guest room, and the tears come. I cannot let you see them.

I rise at dawn, leave quietly. I never see you again, except in dreams.

The shell holds a universe of other shells.

Another Airplane

Driving to the airport, I count seven red-tailed hawks. Some are perched on telephone poles or sitting on the golden field in the morning light. Others circle above. Must be the time of year, I think, time of day.

I fly back to Orlando through a vapory fog, furrows of golden land unfurling below. This is your word: *unfurl*. The plane's engine, a constant wind. And then the night comes, with its patchwork of lights.

I look at my phone and read the last messages you sent me:

You can't stop living just because you might be dying
For as long as we can in life, we must, we MUST, write.
Love you!
I'm losing my coordination
It's the tumors
Love back
☺

The Crow

Among your friends I cannot help but look for you. And there you are: your picture is very large, and it's on a stand at the front, and I wonder what you would think about that. *Very funereal,* I can hear you say. But it's a nice picture, isn't it?

Later Brian asks me if I want the picture. In his well of loss, he can't see that offering me this giant picture of you to carry home on the airplane is funny. Or maybe it's me and it isn't funny at all. Or maybe it's that we have always thought the same things are funny and I still want that. I know it is sweet and he means it because he is already trying to figure out how he might wrap it so I can carry it onto the airplane. I want so badly to tell you this.

So many things I want to tell you. And I do.

Someone was playing bagpipes, and it has just started to rain. Spanish moss hangs in green shawls from the oak trees above our heads, and the resurrection ferns come back to life, remembering elasticity and shape. A crow calls from the rain-drenched sky. I crane my neck to see it in the elbow of a branch.

Then the rain lets up, and the sun comes. In my memory the man on the bagpipes plays "Here Comes the Sun," but I don't know if that's right. That's how memory works: eventually, it becomes real, whether it happens or not.

I say a few words, then read one of your poems. My voice cracks. *I am becoming bird.*

The Hummingbird

It has been three months. It is raining—unseasonably warm for mid-December in Tahoe, where I live. I read your poems in the gray light of the morning—new poems, so full of flying things. I look up to watch the flames flicker orange in the fireplace—what to do with this aliveness?

Albert Camus says, "After a while, you could get used to anything." But I'm not so sure that's true.

When the brain tumors take away your language, you still find a way to speak in metaphor. You make jewelry for your friends.

You make me three necklaces and a pin. I do not know about them until after you've gone. The pin is a world, with sun, moon, stars, and, at the edge of the earth, a small angel. One necklace is a compass. Another is an empty timepiece: inside, a smaller pocket watch, a book, a bee, and a hummingbird. With these you are telling me what you want for me, what to do with my small clock of time.

I understand what you want me to know, can read it all, except the hummingbird. I want to ask you. There is the obvious metaphor of the birds and the bees, but I do not understand the hummingbird until later, when my mother is dying and she tells me this: *When I'm gone, I will come to you as a hummingbird.*

How could you have known?

The Goose

The last necklace looks like a porthole, with a pink-petaled flower on one side and a round-eyed bird on the other. I try to see a hawk inside the blown glass, but you say, *That isn't a hawk. It's a goose, silly!* And we laugh.

The Egret

The next time I see Brian, we are at a writing residency in Jamaica. I go to hug him, and a white flash erupts from a palm: an egret sailing into the night sky. I am too shy to tell him I think it must have been you.

Firefly

Later that night, when I tell Brian my mother is dying, bright flashes spiral across the lawn. He says, "That's Ilyse, checking in with you." You are there at the crease, where the world beneath the world shows through.

I see you, firefly.

The Angel

I am home, looking out the window, and it's raining again. The pine and fir trees shift in the wind. A silvery mist hides the lake and sky. The raven is back, croaks from a branch. I rise from my chair, walk to the window. Raindrops chart rivers down the glass.

Another raven answers the call, then swoops through the wind and lands on a lower bough. The branches of a naked aspen are white, like bones. The dog sleeps by the fire.

It's nearly Christmas, and I think about the lighted angel we placed at the top of our tree when I was a child and how I always made sure the other angels hung from nearby branches below. That way, I told my mother, they are close enough so when they talk to her, the angel above will still be able to hear her friends.

The rain turns finally to snow.

A Kiss for the Dying

Mother has been told she's dying. Maybe three months, the internist shrugs. He listens to her heart, the lungs filled with tumors. Then he says, "What you have is very bad."

Mother pulls a face at him, and I try not to laugh.

When the pulmonologist walks into the room, Mother asks, "Have you heard? I'm a goner."

He doesn't answer, and he takes her pulse. "It's very fast," he says and then tells her there's a nerve in her neck and if he presses on it, the heart will slow down.

It works, and Mother says, "You should go to Vegas," meaning he might take his magic trick on the road. But he only hears "vagus," and he says, "Very good! That is your vagus nerve."

We all laugh, except the doctor.

Over the past few months, Mother has lost her sense of humor, and when I asked her why, she said, "Because nothing is funny anymore." She hadn't been feeling well, thought it was her heart, wondered why she wasn't getting better. But once she was diagnosed with extensive small cell lung cancer, the most aggressive form of lung cancer, everything is funny again, even things that aren't. Like the man in the hospital room next door, wailing to anyone who passes his room, "Nurse, help me. Nurse? Doctor? Help me."

Mother is getting a blood transfusion, and by the second bag of blood, she starts imitating him: *Nurse! Help me!*

He is constipated, and she is dying, so her mockery only seems fair. Even our nurse, who has tired of this man's constant moaning, laughs with us.

Before I leave her room, I walk to the side of her hospital bed, and I bend down under the fluorescent lights to kiss her. The skin on her forehead is sometimes dry and papery beneath my lips; sometimes it is cold and damp. I kiss her, and I say the same thing every time. I say, "Don't die, okay?"

And she says, "No, I won't."

And we laugh.

Later I ask Mother over the phone if she remembers her first kiss with my father. She laughs and says, "Of course I do."

"Tell me."

"Well," she says, "it was after our first date. We went to the beach, and when he dropped me off, he kissed me."

"Did he ask you first?"

"No, but he knew."

"How?"

"A woman has a way of showing it. You should know," she says. "But more than that first kiss. I knew I wanted to marry him the minute I met him. It's strange to me now. But I just knew."

Then Mother asks me if I remember my first kiss.

I tell her the oleander rustled in the hot Santa Ana winds and the asphalt melted beneath my Keds. Then his tongue entered my mouth like a surprise. I could not have pictured that development when I kissed my pillow, practicing for the moment. I didn't know slipping a tongue into another's mouth was a thing. I had heard of French kissing and thought it meant tilting your head and kissing for a long time. Or a kind of kissing invented in France—something foreign and mysterious. I wasn't sure, but I wouldn't have guessed it involved the tongue.

I didn't know that within a few days, this boy would tell me it was over. Or that this first kiss, and the kisses that followed, would do nothing to save me from the horrors of junior high school. And after this first kiss, everything else would come far too quickly.

I knew only the kiss tasted like Jolly Rancher sour apple candy and everything else disappeared—my eyes shut tight to the afternoon sun of my own becoming.

We are in the hospital again, and I ask Mother to tell me about the first time she kissed me. The fluorescent lights double in the glossed linoleum floors.

"It wasn't right away. They took you away and cleaned you. I couldn't wait for the nurses to bring you back, and when they did, I kissed you."

"Where?" I ask, but I already know the answer. Another patient scuffs the hallway with a walker.

"On the forehead. And your father did too. And you had this blue vein that sort of popped out there. Your father was so worried about it. But I knew it would be fine, and it was."

There are pictures around her house of Mother and me when I am little, and in some we are kissing. There are no such pictures of me and my father. I do not remember ever kissing him. And since I wasn't there when he died, I never kissed him goodbye.

Sometimes he comes back to me in dreams, but by the time I reach him, he's already gone: in this way he has died countless deaths.

On my way out of Mother's hospital room, I rub foamy hand sanitizer into my hands, a ritual that has come to feel something like prayer. And next door the howling and the smell of blood and urine, disinfectant and shit. I walk the shiny halls and then come back to her room and leave again, and every time I go, I say it. I kiss her goodbye on the forehead, and I say, "Don't die," and she doesn't.

It's only funny if she stays alive.

Bone & Skin

1.

I tell you I'm getting a tattoo to cover my scars. Some kind of tree, perhaps, the branches reaching across one scar, the roots wrapped around another. A living thing. An ancient bristle-cone, a saguaro, a juniper, purple with berries. "You're allergic to juniper," you say, and I nod. I do not ask, "But isn't that the point?" And it isn't true—I don't really want the tattoo. I trace the scars with a fingertip, the thin, hard edge remembering the blade. The evidence of fracture, wound, fragility. The fine white light, the pucker of skin, the pink star where the bone broke free.

2.

I am crying again, and you tell me you're worried about me, that I carry too much grief. "You let it accumulate," you say, "instead of letting it go." Sometimes I think about this and I am angry. Other times I wonder if you're right. I know with each new loss, there's a heaviness in me, dressed in too many layers, wrong for the weather. You ask, "But what will happen to you as the years wear on? There's nothing but loss ahead." I do not say holding onto these losses scares me less than trying to let them go. I do not say the weight of them prevents me from floating away and disappearing. I do not say I am more alive—with pain, yes, but alive—every time someone else I love has died.

3.

Sometimes when we're making love, I can't help but think about our skeletons, foundations beneath flesh: the jutted pelvis, iliac crest, sculpted like a seashell. Your now-fleshy hands grasp the mantle of my hips—the skeletons, fibrous and calcified, will soon enough be stripped clean without the canvas of skin, red strip of muscle, the jellied yellow tissue. These woven bones, at last, shining naked. The hips, ribs, and skull—the inside finally out. The eye sockets emptied—no longer a lookout. Like the last page of a book, holding the air of already having seen. Emptied of recognition— emptied of this moment, this brief intermission of tension and delight, the silver orgasmic quiver of the almost already dead.

4.

My mother once told me her pain felt better only when she cried out—her groaning swelled to howl as the cancer ate away her vertebrae. When the pitch of her pain startled me, my own body betrayed me too—I had to stifle a laugh. I understand the element of surprise can shake us into tears or to laughter, but still—there is no way not to burn with shame.

5.

When I cry out in pain in the small hours following the accident, you do not laugh. But you want me to stop. "I'm afraid the neighbors will think I'm beating you." That makes me laugh, between my cries, even if it isn't funny. My mother was right—the screaming gives the body its distraction. And also the metaphors: I tell you the pain is a shooting star—a hot, white bolt ripping through skin and bone. It is the inside of a creature's jaw, the crunch of locked fangs. You beg me to take the pain pills, but I refuse the dull throb, wanting instead the sharp truth of it—the involuntary breathless howl, present and primal—the laughter, orgasm, tears.

Wearing Her Eye Shadow

My friend's husband, Brian, said he had something for me, then handed over a bag of Ilyse's makeup. Eye shadow had broken open, pinkish-purple dust coating the contents. He said, "Fuck! I should've been more careful with it. I hope there's something you can use." It took Brian three years after she died to part with this. He doesn't know makeup expires or that people shouldn't wear each other's. Later my husband said, "Throw that away." I did, but the next day, while alone, I fished the bag from the garbage. Her eyeliner is my shade. I'm wearing it now.

A Love Letter to My Hometown
after the Shooting

If there were a picture in the dictionary of "American suburban life," it would be of Thousand Oaks, with its rolling hills and oak trees, its luxury car dealerships and shopping malls. I found all that safety stifling when I was growing up, so after college I didn't return like some of my childhood friends did. I said, "I'll never live in the suburbs again," and that has proven mostly true—until my mother was diagnosed with terminal cancer and I returned to my hometown to care for her. I had tried to persuade her to move up to Lake Tahoe with me, but she wasn't having it. She had lived in Thousand Oaks for nearly forty years, and she wanted to die there.

In the months I lived there with her, I walked with my dog through the manicured neighborhoods, passing the gated communities in Sunset Hills, returning to her community, where all the stucco houses look exactly the same. In the fall a murder of crows caw from the sycamores, and in the spring bunnies hop across the greenbelts.

I drove the familiar roads, past my elementary, middle, and high schools, on my way to pick up my mother's medications and shop for her groceries. I strolled through The Oaks shopping mall, lit with holiday lights and decorations, looking for gifts. When my mother felt well enough, we went to the library and local park together, watching the ducks and the turtles, looking for the beauty in the world. And we found it.

Last year, when the bank called to tell me the sale of my childhood home was complete, the escrow officer said, "Congratulations!" I started to cry. And like all people who surprise others with their unexpected tears, I apologized, saying, "It's just really hard."

Although I shouldn't have done it, a few months ago, when I was back in town for my high school reunion, I drove by our house, the house I didn't know I loved until it was gone. It felt like the end of an era, but my childhood and teenage years—roller-skating and track meets, hiking in Wildwood and ice blocking on the Sunset Hills golf course—are still there in the hometown that lives in the dwelling place of my memory.

This is all to say that the safety of Thousand Oaks may have felt stifling to me when I was a young person, looking for adventure beyond my parents' house; now, after the murder of twelve people in another mass shooting has made the community's name a household word, like so many other American cities and towns, I see I relied on it—even if I wasn't going to live there, something about knowing it was there was important to me. My first kiss was in the parking lot of The Oaks mall. The friendships I made at Thousand Oaks High School have lasted into my adulthood. Both my parents died in this city.

The mayor of Thousand Oaks said that if this can happen there—meaning the Borderline Bar mass shooting, where those twelve people died—then it can happen anywhere. I always already knew that, or at least I thought I did when it happened in other places, places close to home but not home exactly.

If my mother were still alive, she would be watching the news on its horrible loop, getting up only during commercials. She'd be checking in with her friends from the local hardware store, where she worked, because some of her young colleagues frequented Borderline. I would tell her to turn off the news, and she would shush me, saying, as she often did when she heard about people who died suddenly: "And they didn't even have a death sentence." What she meant was she had been given three months to live after being diagnosed with cancer, and she herself had accepted this death sentence. During every month she lived after that, and she was still there, sitting on the couch, alive, she would ask, when she heard of sudden death, "It's incredible, isn't it? No one even told them they were going to die."

But here in America, we're all living with a death sentence, one we also have come to accept. Death awaits us at movies and nightclubs, at our elementary schools and colleges, in our synagogues, our mosques, and our churches. The very thing that some of us argue keeps us free and safe—our right to own guns—has become our terminal diagnosis, and we can't escape it, not even in the safest city in America. Most of us go about our lives, pretending we will stay safe until the next terrible shooting, because it feels like there's very little we can do about it. The way helplessness becomes complacency.

When my mother was dying, she said, "Don't talk to me about the cancer. Stop saying *the word*, all right?"

Around her I never said *cancer* and *chemotherapy* and *end of life*. I pretended because I could do nothing about the destruction of Mother's body. I could only hold space and bear witness and make tea. It wasn't denial, exactly, but a silent pact that we would not talk about the inevitable. We sat across from each other at the oncologist's office as she lay back into the big chair, a steady drip of etoposide and carboplatin delivered to her veins through clear, plastic tubing. The poison, they had said, was the cure. But we knew that wasn't true either. But what were we to do? Waiting it out and hoping for the best wasn't going to be enough. Mother knew the chemotherapy wouldn't cure metastatic disease, but still she asked, "What am I supposed to do? Sit around and do nothing?"

I drove Mother home from chemotherapy, past the tidy greenbelts, the oak-scattered hillsides. Hers was a death sentence, as she called it, we could do nothing about, but even so, doing nothing wasn't an option. I pointed out a hawk overhead, the light glinting red off its tail. For the time being we were there together, struggling toward something, and I suppose that's where everything always begins.

The Red Canoe

In memory of Robert Greene

"When it's my time," you always said, "push me downriver in the red canoe."

Instead, we sit with the other slumped memory care residents and sing karaoke: "Mustang Sally," "Peggy Sue," and "Little Darlin'." The doctor says you might retain the ability to read long after nearly everything else goes. You still know the words by heart.

Colorful African fish hide in between the rocks and reeds of a bubbling tank. Finches flit back and forth in a glass cage. You are pale, and I wonder how long it's been since you were outside.

You went through this with your own mother and accept it is happening to you, but you worry this will happen to your children and their daughters. The thought makes you cry. But that's gone, too, because your brain's mosaic is now moment and shard without cement—too disconnected for depression. And soon, the doctor says, you will lose the ability to smile, which is hard to imagine until it isn't.

Someone asks you, joking, if you would like green eggs and ham. You say, "Yes, I would like some bog and gam." For now you smile. And so do we.

You start sentences about fixing things or going fishing, and then the words scatter like confetti, so you pat your baby doll named Katie. (Who named her? No one seems to know.) "She likes that," you say. The woman seated on the couch next to you holds a stuffed dog. She smiles and says "Why, hello," and then later frowns and says, "It's time for me to go home. Home. Home." There's a shift in her anxious face, and she loses track of what she's saying, smooths the dog's gray fur, and smiles again, saying, "Please, do come again." We agree, though we will soon be on our way to board an airplane and then another.

I worry when you put Katie down someone will pick her up, mistake her for his own. But this never happens. Everyone knows whose doll or stuffed toy belongs to whom.

At the family meeting the doctor explains the three ways you will likely die: infection, trauma, or air hunger. Your oldest daughter says, "But Pa isn't ready to go. I asked him if he wanted to meet Jesus, and he said no." A brother-in-law, also a doctor, wonders why the other ailments are being treated—insulin for diabetes, antibiotics for infections. An argument about ethics ensues, and the middle daughter tells her doctor-husband, with her eyes, to be quiet. I only nod, hearing it all but saying nothing, married into the family. But I wonder, *Is this Pa's red canoe?*

You once told me you never wanted to be a burden. But your oldest daughter claims she speaks a common language with you, understands what you want. She visits you more than we do. She carries with her a baggie of her own prescription drugs, and I wonder how many pills would be enough to send Pa downriver.

When Gammy—that's what the grandchildren called your wife—was alive, we sat together by the window. Black-capped chickadees fluttered like eyelashes on the seed-dappled snow. A tangle of birch branches, a gray web against white sky. She told me, "He's not the boy I married. The doctors call it cognitive impairment. They don't want to say dementia or Alzheimer's. He can answer the five questions they ask him, but they don't live with him, watch as he searches for his tools or his jacket." But the tools are under the trapdoor, along with what he's supposed to do before the train leaves, whether or not this is his blue jacket. "I know I shouldn't be drinking," Gammy told me. "I don't know why I do it. It's dangerous for someone like me. But look outside," she said, "it's snowing again." We watched as you worked in the yard with your youngest son, my husband, despite the snow. And the bird tracks were covered, one flake at a time.

Years earlier, when the signs became clear, you took up drawing as a way to exercise your mind. You sketched a picture of a canoe in charcoal—in it, a boy and his father. The picture now hangs on our library wall. My husband says, "I think that's Pa and me. Do you think so too?"

I say I think so. I don't say that the black-and-white canoe—it's meant to be red.

Traveling with Ghosts

Normandy, France, 2003

I am very sick, maybe the flu, but I am determined to make the most of Paris, to live, as I have begun thinking about it, an extraordinary life. The next day will be my thirty-third birthday. I have left my husband, Craig, and my lover, David, goes to the café with me; we eat off small white dishes in the lamplight. I'm not feeling well, but I'm stubborn. "You shouldn't drink wine if you don't feel well," he says and orders a Coke.

I know how to say I would like a glass of red wine in French. And I do. Two women walk by, both wearing short skirts and tall boots. Then two police officers skate by on Rollerblades. I point them out, trying to change the subject.

We go see Moulin Rouge! because I want to do everything quintessential Paris, even if that means the touristy things too. By the time we arrive at the show, which starts very late, I'm flushed and woozy with fever and wine. Champagne corks pop in the dark of the sunken theater. The women are topless and sometimes even bottomless but also in costume, with elaborate feathers, beads, and sparkling things. They dance on tightropes and underwater. One woman swims with a boa constrictor. They clutch the bars of cages, whirl around poles, kick up stilettoed heels. I am in awe of them. I do not turn to my lover to see what he thinks.

Walking back through the October fog, he says, "Did you know that was going to be a nudie show?"

I don't remember whether or not I knew. I only remember thinking it was all part of the experience, and who cared? Maybe I say, "Tits and flash, feathers and ass," to try to lighten the mood. Or more likely, I ask, "Why are you such a prude?"

It is late, into the small hours, but it's now my birthday, and I want to stop somewhere for a glass of wine. "Yes, *another* glass of wine," I might say. I want to sit in a café outdoors, watch the shadows of the trees, like the old man in Hemingway's "A Clean, Well-Lighted Place."

"It's so late, and we have that Normandy tour tomorrow," he says. We walk back along the shimmering Seine in silence. The linden trees hold tight to leaves that flutter against their branches.

That night I have three dreams. In one, my house is on fire, and I have to grab what I want, but I don't have enough time. In another, Melmoth the Wanderer is my lover. In the last one, I dream of the man who won't become my next husband for another ten years.

The next morning I feel even worse than before, as if, I tell him, a truck has backed up and dumped bricks onto me. "I can't go," I say. "You go without me."

"We always do whatever you want, and this is the one thing I wanted to do. And I've already paid for two."

I squeeze into the small van with the others. I can't stop coughing and blowing my nose. I still feel terrible about going, about giving in to David. About possibly giving other travelers the flu.

We travel through the green countryside north to Normandy, to walk among the dead, the ghosts of war. My stuffed head makes everything seem surreal. We walk onto the beach, and I try to picture those young men gunned down at the shore. I listen to the waves and for the echo of gunshots and of howls on the wind. A thin white line separates the sky from the horizon. The concrete bunkers hunch in the sand, rebar bends toward a gray sky. Utah, Omaha, Gold, Juno, and Sword. I ask the guide where the names come from. He says they are the Allied code names, tells us a general asked two soldiers where they were from and they used these names. "The others," he says, "were named by the British and Canadians for fish—goldfish, swordfish, jellyfish, but jelly was changed to Juno because Churchill disapproved of the name Jelly for a beach where so many men would die."

We wander La Pointe du Hoc, and the guide tells us it is the "fake-out place," where the Germans placed decoy guns and the Allies climbed the sea cliffs. The land is a patchwork of bullet holes and barbed wire. Then the rain comes, the kind that blasts sideways and creates its own wilderness. It turns our umbrellas inside out, rendering them useless.

It is time for lunch, and we head to a restaurant in a very old stone building. We are offered wine but both decline. We are seated next to a psychiatrist from New York City who tells me when he travels with his wife, they go see the same sights on different days. Today she is at the museums. Tomorrow she will take this tour, and he will go to museums. I wonder about this for a long time.

We load back into the van and head to the Normandy American Cemetery, where 9,387 fallen are buried. Wet grass, a glassy green, soaks our shoes and the bottoms of our jeans as we walk past cross after white cross. More limitless gray sky. David wants to find the Star of David markers at the cemetery. We find one such marker, and I take his picture. He is wearing a black raincoat; the backdrop is a foggy sky and an electric-green lawn. I look back on the photo now, wonder why he's smiling. I don't remember thinking about it then. Only knowing, always, I was never Jewish enough—the father's side, the wrong side. I do not remember if he asked me if I wanted a photograph, but if he did, I must have declined because no such picture exists.

When I was a little girl, I learned about the Holocaust in school. The detail that stuck with me most was that Nazis made socks from hair, lampshades from the skin, of Jews. I told my father this. I do not remember laughing, but I must have been laughing because my father shouted at me. "It isn't funny. My cousins—your cousins—were murdered there." I must have been seven or eight, too young to separate something that sounded funny to me from something so horrific in its meaning. "God damn it," he said. "Don't you know there are people out there who would hate you for being Jewish?" I didn't ask what he meant or who these cousins were. I remember only the deep shame.

Years later, after everyone I could ask was already dead, I spent hours on ancestry websites. I followed branching family lines and messaged strangers with whom I shared DNA. I found their names, and I cried: Max, Rosa, and Manfred Bottstein were on a late transport to Auschwitz. Manfred was twenty—five years younger than my father had been at the time. Deported October 26, 1942, from Berlin. My grandfather's cousin, his wife. Their son. I do not know if they went straight to the gas. I only know they never returned. But it's important I write their names these eighty years later. It isn't a stone symbol on a green lawn, but it's something: Max, Rosa, Manfred. Their extraordinary lives cut short.

My father changed his last name from Bottstein to Roberts out of fear. My real last name is a palimpsest; the traces remain.

Mád, Hungary, 2011

I have spent the summer on a writing fellowship in Prague. My friend Brenda has come to visit me. She works as a distributor in the wine industry, so we have traveled to Hungary to tour the vineyards where the famous Royal Tokaji is made.

We are having a wine-soaked lunch after our winery tour. The hostess says, "This town used to be full of Jews before the war, but now there's not a single Jewish family left."

I do not remember how this came up in our conversation. Perhaps I had asked about the eighteenth-century synagogue.

Our hostess from the winery holds up the last of the bottle and asks, "More wine?"

I nod, and she pours the dry Furmint in my glass. "And the wine here"—she shows us the bottle so we can admire the label—"was originally made by a Jewish family. That was a long time ago, of course." After a beat, she adds, "But the ghosts remain."

I watch as a stork takes off from a brick chimney across the street. Every house has constructed cages over their rooftops, mesh to prevent the storks from nesting on the chimneys, but still every chimney as far as I can see holds a stork's nest. "So many storks," I say.

"Oh, yes. They are lovely, no? For us they are a sign of springtime. We are always happy to see them come back in March or April. You can see where the childhood story comes from about storks bringing babies down the chimney."

I nod, agree they are lovely, and take a bite of halászlé, a paprika fish stew.

"So the Jews," I ask, "did they happen to hide in the wine caves when the Nazis came?"

"I don't know that," our hostess says. "I do know they were rounded up, confined to the synagogue for three days, and then walked out to the tracks and put on the train for the ghettos in Sátoraljaújhely before they were transported."

"But before that," I ask, "did any of them try to hide in the wine caves?"

"I don't know."

At the risk of sounding foolish, I say, "I felt something in those caves. I don't know what, but there was an energy. And I kept getting these blurry spots when I took photographs."

At that Brenda shakes her head and says, "You have such an imagination, girl!"

I laugh and say, "It was probably nothing." This is Brenda's work trip, after all, and I don't want to embarrass her.

When you grow up with a Jewish parent who lived through the Holocaust, the thought is ingrained: where would I hide? My father had made it clear: *There are people who hate you.* It wouldn't matter in these circumstances that you are the wrong half. You are both too Jewish and not Jewish enough.

The child's mind, especially if she has read and reread *The Diary of Anne Frank*, goes straight for the hiding place: Where would I hide if I had to? And then later, who would be brave enough to hide me? Or maybe, who loves me enough?

Royal Tokaji is known as liquid gold, or "the king's wine," and comes from the oldest classified wine region in Europe. Our guide tells us this famous gold-colored dessert wine comes from grapes that have shriveled on the vine due to a mold called botrytis, or "noble rot." Even the decomposition is cloaked with royal adjectives.

The wine is low in alcohol but rich and sweet. It's perfect with a dessert of chocolate or aged gouda and fruit, we are told, or for leisurely sipping, the way we have enjoyed it that morning. Because of Brenda's job, we were treated to a walk through the vineyards, a private tasting and tour, and then a decadent five-course lunch at a restaurant in town.

After tasting these kingly wines in the vineyard, we descended into the wine caves. We entered a small hatch and walked down concrete steps. Fluorescent lamps affixed to the low, arching ceiling lighted the way down steep ramps. We were met with the smell of charred oak, fermenting grapes, aging wines, and a cool underground earthiness. We followed our guide down through the labyrinth of caves, lined with thousands of oak barrels. Mold coated the walls in a gauzy net, like a bridal veil, only black. The guide told us these cellars were built in the mid-sixteenth century and explained the aging process for the wines.

I took photographs, but every digital image was smudged with blue and purple halos. I kept playing with the settings on my SLR camera, and still I couldn't get a photo without these diaphanous blobs in the frame. Even when I wasn't shooting into light, I couldn't get a picture of the caves without the blurry spots. *Orbs*, I thought, *oh shit*.

A few weeks earlier I had taken a ghost tour in Prague. It was just for fun because I didn't really believe in ghosts—had not yet been haunted the way I would be in later years.

I took the tour with two friends I had met at the Prague writing fellowship. We followed a guide with a huge umbrella, which we joked about and called "the red umbrella of death." The tour wound around the ancient center of Prague, ending in the dungeon of the castle. My new friends Julia, Travis, and I took turns trying to scare each other, making fun of the ghost tour.

When the guide told us to shine our cameras into the light and notice the orbs—the ghosts—in our digital images, we laughed again, repeating, "Do you see the orbs?" We knew they had been caused by shooting into bright lights.

And now in the dark caves, I captured nothing but orbs.

I hurried to catch up with Brenda and our guide. We passed large Hungarian oak barrels and smaller French ones. Brenda asked the guide if we could try some wine from the barrel, and he said, "But of course."

He pulled out a thief, which is like a turkey baster for wine, and drew some of the golden liquid from a barrel and released it into a glass. Brenda took a sip, holding it on her tongue before she swallowed, and then handed the glass to me to do the same. As I sipped the wine, our guide asked, "Do you know what it's called when we come to these barrels and some has evaporated and we must top it off?"

"Angel's share," Brenda said, noticeably pleased she knew the answer.

"Yes, very good." He put the bung back into the small hole in the top of the wine barrel. "And this is a wine that would surely make the angels sing aloud in praise." He swirled the golden liquid in his glass and said, "Wine is about history and memory. It requires time and knowledge. It is a lovely drink, and for me nothing compares. What does this wine remind you of?"

"Melon, honey, and apricots," I said.

As I said the word *apricot*, he pointed at me and said, "Exactly. Mixing the plum and apricot jam over the fire when I was a child. This reminds me. Even today. And the dry wines we tried? It is like when we were children and would pick up a stone from the river and suck on it."

Brenda said, "Yes, exactly."

I had never sucked on a wet stone, so I stayed quiet and smiled.

The guide told us these wines would go on to age for fifty years or more in the bottle. "They go from fresh fruit to dried fruit. And then tea leaf and cigar." He laughed and said, "The way some marriages will age." Then he asked, "Would you like to try more?"

We both shook our heads. We had tried enough wine.

"Very well. Let's head back to the surface of the earth then, shall we?"

We followed him, and I stopped to take a few more pictures, but still the blobs. The orbs. Brenda and the guide walked ahead. That's when I felt the draft. At first the caves were a relief from the hot sun above, but now it was so cold, I shivered. I jogged to catch up to them and asked, "Where's that draft coming from?"

Brenda said she didn't feel it, adding, "But you know me. Always hot."

Our guide said, "There is no draft. We are deep underground."

I nodded even though I still felt it. I pulled my light sweater tighter around me and crossed my arms against my chest. I wondered if maybe it was just the wine or because I was so very tired from our early-morning train ride from Budapest. I followed them to the entrance of the cave, climbed the ladder, and felt the warmth pour over me. My eyes adjusted to the light, and I was happy to see the sun.

I didn't think much more about it.

Not until we are having lunch and I hear about the Jews and I blurt out feeling the draft and seeing the orbs to our hostess. Even though Brenda has dismissed me and my active imagination, our hostess says, "Sometimes that can happen . . . those strange and eerie feelings." She looks out the windows, and I follow her line of sight, watch a stork take off. I take another sip of wine, set down my glass, close my eyes, and try to conjure a memory, not from my own life but from a deeper past.

Nothing comes.

I open my eyes, and outside the window a stork takes off. The black wing feathers look like long fingers. I gasp at its black and white beauty, at the way such a large bird can glide through the sky between slow and measured wingbeats.

Friending the Dead

When the friend request comes in—Kenny Williams wants to be your friend—you don't have to flip through the Rolodex of your mind to place the name with that pinkish face, red wavy hair, and tooth-gapped smile.

With a shaky hand, you click over to his wall, and there it is: RIP *Kenny Williams.*

Kenny Williams is dead. But he wants to be your friend. You realize a cousin, or perhaps one of his five children, had seen your mutual friends. Maybe you have come up on the sidebar under *People You May Know* because you went to the same junior high, listed the same hometown.

He wants to be your friend, but it isn't really him. You are not his friend. The boy who tormented you is live on Facebook but dead. You feel relieved, something approaching happy, because he is dead. Then you wonder: *What's wrong with me?*

You haven't seen him in more than thirty years. But still, you carry it.

The junior high classroom had been arranged by last name, so Mr. Ballard, the ancient life sciences teacher, could remember who was who. R got seated next to W. And we were required to share a worm, a frog, and a fetal pig with our partner during dissections. My partner, Kenny Williams, was more interested in scrambling the frog's guts, throwing the worm in my hair, and pulling out the fetal pig's heart and mashing it between his fingers.

That was the best of it.

Between botched dissections, Kenny whispered, "I bet you don't know what a blow job is."

"Yes, I do."

"Do not."

"Do too." I was not the kind of girl who liked to admit her ignorance.

"If you know what it is, will you give me one?" he asked.

"Sure." A blow job sounded like a lollipop.

Then everyone in my seventh grade class would be told, by Kenny Williams himself, that I wanted to suck dick. That's when I learned what a blow job really was, though at first I didn't believe it. Could it be true anyone would actually put a penis in a mouth? I had not yet been kissed, and I had no idea a blow job was in the repertoire of the possible.

By the middle of the year, Kenny passed me notes:

I know you want to fuck me.

Your tits are hard. Thinking about me?

Nice jeans. I can see your coozie.

We were eleven years old.

I asked Mr. Ballard if I could move seats, but he told me we don't always get what we want in life, and my last name began with R, so I had to sit at the back of the room in the second-to-last row next to Mr. Williams. He couldn't go changing seats for everyone who wanted to move or didn't like her dissection partner, now could he? I had to learn to work with other children, no matter the differences.

What if I had told Mr. Ballard exactly what was happening to me? Would I have been asked what had I done to attract this kind of attention? Wasn't it always the girl who was to blame?

I didn't have it in me at eleven to doubt the alphabetized seating chart, to see Mr. Ballard as the accomplice he was. How many teachers are ignoring it, even today, while girls and boys are being terrorized at the backs of classrooms?

I know now that eleven-year-old girl was not to blame.

But there's something in me still left of her, something that feels like maybe it was my fault. Because of my silence? Because of my confusion about my own burgeoning sexuality? Because though I found Kenny's advances terrifying, that terror was somehow, inexplicably, exciting? It was like getting sick on the Tilt-a-Whirl at the fair—a thrilling nausea. And no one to blame but yourself. You'd traded in your ticket for that ride.

By the end of the year, Kenny not only passed me dirty notes; he snapped my bra (hard), snatched at my early-developing breasts, and reached for the crotch of my purple Gloria Vanderbilt jeans, which fit tighter as the year wore on. And when he got a hard-on, which was often, he would grab my hand and try to put it on the lump in his OP corduroy shorts. He'd say, *You're such a tease. Because of you, my cock's hard.*

I was the first of my friends to get her period, wear a bra, and by the seventh grade, I already filled a C cup. I thought Kenny Williams's advances were my fault for developing early. I started wearing tops with frills along the front and long skirts and dresses, as if I were auditioning for a part on *Little House on the Prairie*. And at lunch every day, I ate a chocolate shake, chocolate chip cookies, and French fries. I gained twenty pounds in a year, and my face bloomed with acne. My breasts and my butt only got bigger. There was no hiding, not even under a layer of preteen fat and prairie dresses.

I had been in the Popular Crowd since the fourth grade when I moved to the suburbs from Los Angeles. Being "in" was a benefit I enjoyed without thinking twice about the possibility I could so easily be out. In the complicated politics of junior high school, you can go from Popular to Misfit overnight, and that's exactly what happened to me. The popular girls were slender with clear complexions. They didn't wear glasses, and they had the right jelly shoes, the kind my mother thought too expensive, and to her credit, they *were* made of plastic.

I started getting crank calls from the girls who had previously wanted me to wear the other half of their BFF necklaces, girls who had passed me notes with hearts over every *i*. Now the notes read:

Fatty four-eyes. You are so fat. How do you fit through the door?
Slut. Everyone knows you want to suck Kenny Williams's cock.
Bitch!

The crank calls became so frequent, my parents had our telephone number changed.

To be my friend would mean social exile, so I became the girl at school who sat alone at lunch, slurping a chocolate shake. None of my teachers took me in like you read about, allowing me to clean their chalkboard erasers at lunch. It seemed even they knew that if they befriended me, there would be adolescent hell to pay.

I finally noticed I wasn't the only outcast, so I made friends with the other misfits, the skinny Diane Poprock, the shy Long Ngo, the mousy Jane Fiedler (who felt sorry for me because her sister had put her up to the crank calls, providing a voice I wouldn't recognize). We clung to each other until it was time for high school, and we went off to different schools, leaving junior high, but not the memories, behind.

Luckily, Kenny Williams went to a different high school— the continuation school for bad boys, I later found out on Facebook—and I never saw him again.

I never once considered his advances were not my fault. This was confirmed in my "slut phase" years later, when I really did suck the cocks of ungrateful boys and men in hopes of being noticed, and maybe even loved, by them.

I once read that dysfunctional boys become violent, while dysfunctional girls get pregnant. Boys want to hurt others; girls set out to destroy themselves. At twenty-two I had a boyfriend who liked to grab my ass. I told him to stop. When he didn't, I cried and told him it made me feel like a slut because I had already slept with too many men. My boyfriend asked, "I'm not going to catch a disease, am I?"

I learned to keep my mouth shut after that, but it would be a long time before I could stand up for myself, reject the labels given to me by a sexist world, one that says, "C'mon, he's only teasing" when someone asks an eleven-year-old girl if she wants to suck dick. The world that has put the word *slut* into the mouths of eleven-year-old girls.

My nieces are girls of eight, eleven, and twelve. They wear pink braces, giggle with each other over secret jokes, awkwardly steal glances of themselves in the mirror. They like playing volleyball, learning ballet, making chocolate chip cookies, trying on different shades of lip gloss, and taking pictures of each other and themselves. I want to see my eleven-year-old self in them: innocent and blameless and beautiful.

I want to forgive my eleven-year-old self for something I know she could not have done.

Thankfully, Facebook didn't exist in my junior high days. Who knows what Kenny Williams would have posted? Who knows what the Popular Girls might have written about me to hasten my middle school ruin? Who knows the ways my misery would have multiplied, taking on a digital life of its own?

Paper notes floated about Los Cerritos Junior High, lipstick scrawled across my locker. But none of it was indelible, except maybe in the improvisation of memory.

In 1983 paper scraps found their way into trash cans. Lipstick on lockers washed off with rain. But the internet sticks. A Facebook wall remains. More indelible even than memory. Facebook: a place where even the dead can make friends. Since he's been dead, Kenny Williams's recent Facebook history shows he has made thirteen new friends and added the Rock-n-Roll Café as a favorite. Someone wrote on his wall, "I miss you, Bro. Why'd you have to go?"

But there he is: Kenny Williams riding a motorcycle. Kenny Williams drinking a beer. Kenny Williams posing with his pit bull on a boat. Kenny Williams smiling next to a dead lion. The verbs always gerunds—riding, drinking, posing, smiling. On the internet he's still there in the present tense. And if he's still there on Facebook, part of me believes he is still out there.

I can see him from the corner of my eye, sitting in the back of the classroom touching himself, staring at me. I can see myself too: I'm the one floating in the cold formaldehyde. I'm the one dissected. In pieces. Eyes frozen open.

Since my girlhood I have been trying to find the antidote for what I believed I had become: *Slut. Cocktease. Bitch.*

I do not like violent films, but I wanted to see *The Girl with the Dragon Tattoo* because the main character is a badass who fights back and wins. I am a badass only in the dark theater of my dreams. In real life I'm still the myopic girl sitting by myself, drowning my confusion in chocolate milkshakes or, these days, red wine.

I'm also the one stalking through the pages of a dead person on Facebook, looking to find out exactly how Kenny Williams died, hoping to find something there that will reveal something of myself to me. When I look at his profile pictures, even though he is bald, puffy-faced, and wearing a long red goatee, I can see the boy-face there. The same redhead complexion and close-set eyes, the same space between the ridged front teeth. I don't want to be happy he's dead at thirty-nine. But there's something about his Facebook page that makes me believe even if I do speak ill of him, he'll be able to defend himself, speak back.

In my morbid need to know, I message the hometown gossip. She's one of the girls who never escaped the suburbia of our adolescence, and she still knows everything about everyone. I ask her how Kenny Williams died, tell her I sat next to him in science. I write, "39—so young," hoping to imply tragedy. She writes back and says she isn't sure but she heard his death had something to do with alcoholism. First, I feel vindicated and then shame for feeling it.

Because there is also this: a little boy in the Facebook pictures, pre–junior high, the smiling four-year-old, clutching his mother's neck. A blameless boy who bears no resemblance to the boy in my mind's eye. Children learn from others, from older people who do bad things to them. Unthinkable things. I know that now. Was there a cousin or a beer-drinking uncle, Kenny Williams? An unhappy childhood, an unhappy ending.

I want to say I finally feel sorry for him, that I have forgiven him, but the truth is I haven't. For now holding on to the hatred feels like a form of protection. But from what? A ghost? Or the part of myself that isn't ready to reconcile her girl-self and her woman-self? Forgiveness would be the convenient lie I tell myself and then tell you. But in the end the lie does no good. I know enough of myself to know I cannot betray myself for long. The best I can offer is this: to forgive is a process, not a verb of being but one of becoming.

DESIRE

Ultimately, it is the desire, not the desired, that we love.

—FRIEDRICH NIETZSCHE

Keep Your Numbers Down

You are taught to flutter your lashes, look sideways over your shoulder. Smile but not too wide. Ask questions, seem interested. Touch his arm but not his leg. Make him want you. But then don't want him. Keep your numbers down. How many is too many? Decide on a number, one that is respectable. Have fun but not too much. No one-night stands. That counts more than double. Count the football player in high school but not the man from the post office nor the air force pilot. Count the president of the fraternity but not his younger brother. Count the prelaw student from your dorm but not the stoner who lived on the corner. Count the ski instructor nearly twice your age but not the ski patroller who liked doing it doggy style. Don't count the Australian whose jumper you refused to return after you saw him making out with another girl at the Coyote Café. Count your friend's brother but not your big brother in the fraternity. Count the Jewish Spanish teacher from Illinois but not the Puerto Rican tour guide who followed you across an island. The artist, the drinker, the surfer, the cowboy, the triathlete, the poet—don't count them. Their names have already been lost. The number is a witching rod, divining your worth.

In Love with the World

When we got back to the apartment, I was still buzzing with the beat of Shakira, the novelty of dancing late into the night at a Spanish club. But David turned to me and said, "I saw how you danced with all those guys."

"What? I danced with my students. And my boss. You're being ridiculous."

"Am I?" He stood in our narrow hallway.

"Yes," I said, wondering at first if he was joking but knowing, even then, he wasn't. I pulled off my earrings and washed my face in the small sink of our tiny bathroom. He stood at the door and said the thing we were both waiting for him to say: "You cheated before. How do I know you won't do it again? Do *you* know you won't do it again?"

I didn't know, but I could see there was no way I could escape this, his lack of trust and the belief that once a cheater, always a cheater. I wiped my face with a hand towel and said, "I don't know. But there's nothing I can say or do that's going to be the right thing if you don't trust me."

I had been offered a job teaching Spanish poetry, film, and wine (a dream job, I know) for a semester in Salamanca, and I invited David to come with me. This seemed like an easy way to try living together, since being elsewhere was all we had ever known as a couple—meeting secretly in Mexico and London and Las Vegas until my divorce with Craig was final. I wanted nothing more than to make it work.

That night I danced to "Hips Don't Lie" in a small, underground club in Salamanca with my students and the director of the school where I taught, and I felt truly happy. I was thirty-three and living the life I had imagined for myself—I had both responsibility and freedom. I'd been chasing happiness, had wanted nothing more than to travel the world. I'd figured out a way to incorporate travel—being elsewhere—into my real life.

I'd managed to convince David he had nothing to worry about in terms of my infidelity. My marriage had been unfulfilling. Infidelity was my way out of an unhappy situation. But still, I felt tentative and insecure around him. One night after class, David and I sat in the café below our Salamanca apartment, and I put down my journal and asked him what he loved about me.

Before we go any further, I know how pathetic this sounds.

David looked up from his novel and said, "I love how smart you are."

The candle between us struggled to stay aflame, and I smiled at him, remembering the way I had fought with my ex. I took a sip of Rioja and felt a renewed sense of our relationship. "What else?" I asked, greedy for his attention.

"I love that you're adventurous."

"I love that about you too," I said. "And spontaneous."

David went back to his book, and I went back to writing in my journal. I ordered Spanish tortilla and olives. The bartender dished out small plates from trays in front of him and handed them to me. "Gracias," I said, trying to get the Castilian lisp right. I had been eating and drinking like this nearly every evening and had gained weight, a lot of weight, but I didn't care, or at least I told myself that because I wanted to experience all of it, including the Spanish food and wine.

"Do you want some?" I asked David, holding up the plate of tortilla, and he shook his head. Then I asked him, "Do you love that I'm a writer?" I had published a handful of poems in small literary journals and was writing a memoir that didn't seem to be going anywhere, but I was beginning to think of myself as a writer, though it was hard to claim that identity—being a writer seemed much more to me than someone who writes.

"No, I don't love you for being a writer," David said, not looking up from his book.

"What? What do you mean?" I took another swallow of wine.

"It takes you away from me, so no, it's not one of the things I love about you." He looked up at me briefly again and then back down at his book.

"But it's me. You can't separate it." I was surprised at how indignant I sounded, but it was one of those things you learn about yourself only when confronted.

"You asked," David said.

I had had issues with my ex-husband, lots of them, but he had accepted this part of me, celebrated it even. The candle burned down to the lip of the wine bottle that held it and went out.

Over the next few days I tried to reason through what David had said. It was true: writing did take me away from him. I wanted to be adored, and didn't that mean I should also adore him? But I was often lost in my own world when he wanted my attention. When I called my mother and told her about this conversation, she stayed quiet until I asked her, "Do you think it's a big deal?"

"You tell me," Mother said.

"I'm not sure." I walked circles around our apartment. I looked out our window, where I could see a small rectangle of the sand-colored cathedral, its spires jutting into a white sky.

"I think," my mother said and paused, "you already know."

I'd cheated on my husband with David in Mexico, and now I couldn't stop myself from trying to make meaning out of a mistake. I had the guilt-fueled notion my actions would be justified if I committed to a relationship with my new lover.

But guilt is a terrible motivation and, in the words of a dear friend, *a waste of an emotion.* And David, who had once been playful, spontaneous, and adoring, had become judgmental and sullen and mistrustful. I had become desperate, trying to make things better between us.

One evening I came home from school and planned a sexy evening with David. I lit candles, put on music, and when I heard David in the hallway, fumbling with his keys to our apartment, I ran to the door, opened it, and said, "You're home!" I was wearing the sexiest lingerie I had brought with me to Spain—a shabby black bra and lacy thong underwear.

He pushed past me as he said, "I'm meeting Ravi at six to play guitar." He didn't look at me. I followed him into our small bedroom, where we had put the double mattress from the living room sofa bed on the floor because the small flat had come with a twin bed. Above the mattress, black mold spread across the slanted walls of the attic apartment. I kept cleaning it off, but still it grew—this was a metaphor for something, I was sure, but I couldn't say what.

"I've been waiting for you," I said, trying to make it obvious I wasn't merely in the middle of dressing, that this is what I had chosen to wear for his homecoming.

He looked at me for a minute, his face still a blank.

"I was hoping we could . . . you know . . ." I sat on the mattress. The walls seemed to collapse into the room, yellow but not cheerful. Splotches of black mold shined in the light of my mood candles.

David's face finally showed a flicker of recognition, which made my face flush with humiliation. "But you're busy. So never mind," I said and got up. I put my robe on, went into the bathroom, and shut the door. I untied my robe and looked in the mirror; I blamed my body. After a steady diet of Spanish tortilla, *jamón*, and Rioja, the clothes I had brought with me were too tight. I had to go shopping, but none of the clothes at the fashionable Zara fit me either. I ended up buying a pair of corduroys and an oversized sweater at H&M, and this outfit became my new uniform. I had told myself it was fine, just part of the experience of living in Spain. Now I stood in the fluorescent lights of the bathroom, and I hated myself.

Why hadn't I been like those thin Spanish ladies who shopped during lunchtime and siesta instead of eating and sleeping?

David left for his guitar date, and I got dressed and went downstairs to the café, where I ate more Manchego, drank more red wine. I couldn't help but see the irony: the word *adultery* implies hot sex, but the sex, which had never been better than mediocre, dwindled to nothing. It felt like my punishment. I no longer wanted the life I had created—a life for which I had broken up a marriage and moved to another continent. What if I wasn't having a fabulous love affair after all? What if I had just fucked up?

I sat down, opened my laptop, and wrote an email to my friend Tiffany. I told her my fairy-tale romance wasn't going as well as I'd hoped. She wrote back, telling me to try to enjoy Europe while I was there, that I would be home soon enough. She was busy planning her own fairy-tale wedding, and I didn't want to bother her with the details, so I wrote back and told her I would.

I don't give up easily, which is to say I don't give up when all evidence suggests I should. I was even more determined to make it work. I filled our weekends with romantic getaways—vacations from our vacation. I wanted to recapture what we felt for each other in Mexico, and every once in a while, there were glimpses—hiking to the top of the cross in San Sebastian, eating fresh fish in Santiago de Compostela, watching the wooden barrels of port float down the Douro River, clapping to the flamenco dancers in the caves of Seville, walking through the courtyards of the Alhambra in the rain.

But it was never enough—that's the thing about the false narratives of fairy tales.

I thought I had been courageous, leaving my husband and setting off across the world. But if I had really been brave, I would have gone alone. Instead of creating the life I yearned for, I used this relationship as a stand-in for what I really wanted, which was the extraordinary life I could only fashion on my own. If I had stopped to think about it, maybe I would have seen that. Instead, I kept going—another gelato, another glass of port, another weekend excursion—always moving, always striving for the elusive happily ever after.

I finished the semester in December, and David and I flew to Italy for the holidays. Any relationship seen through an Italian lens seemed hopelessly romantic, or at least the way it all sounded—Italy for the holidays!—made me believe I really was living my best life, when what I was doing was trying to cover deceit with an elaborate and strained metaphor, a story about my life I kept telling myself in order to keep going.

And that's how we decided David would move back to Lake Tahoe with me in January. Looking out from the Ponte Vecchio in Florence, he said, "I have a year sabbatical, and we have to go for it. I'll go back to graduate school in Reno, and we can see how we do in the real world."

When I said, "This *is* the real world," David shook his head like I couldn't possibly know what I was saying.

And the "real world" experiment didn't last long—twenty days to be exact.

I came home from skiing to find David's car, the one that had arrived days earlier on the back of a truck from Illinois, had been packed up. "If you hadn't gone skiing today, I wouldn't be leaving," he said. "I decided that if you went skiing today, I was leaving." It had snowed more than a foot the night before—a powder day. When it comes to skiing fresh snow, I can be a very selfish woman indeed, something avid skiers understand. And David knew enough about me to know this: he had devised a test for me he knew I would fail.

And it was never about the skiing. David believed I would cheat on him because I had cheated on my first husband with him. He didn't know this, or maybe he did, but it's only so long before you become what someone already believes you are: it's easy to be untrustworthy when you are not trusted. I cheated, and then I cheated again: the first time was on my husband with David; then again on David with Craig—a palindrome of desire and shame.

One night, a week before David ended up leaving, I called him and told him I'd had too much wine with my writing group, that I couldn't drive home and I was staying with a friend. David offered to come get me, and I said no; it was snowing, and I was fine where I was. The wine part was probably true—a way to quiet my inner voice, which was telling me I had made a mistake. Why had I agreed to David coming home with me? I wanted to assign meaning to the affair, to believe I had broken up my marriage for good reason.

But I didn't stay at my friend's house that night. I walked the two blocks from her house to the house I had once shared with my ex, the one we co-owned and I still paid half the mortgage on. The streetlamps glowed through the falling snow, and the ice on the road shined like glass. The cold air's grip felt elastic.

Craig had heard I was back in town, so when I showed up at the door, he didn't seem surprised to see me. I walked across the hardwood floors I had loved, and he asked me if I wanted a drink. I said no. I don't remember if anything else was said.

I walked into the bedroom we had shared: a way to even the score, making sure everyone lost. I shouldn't have done it, but I did it just the same. And now it's another point on the plot of my life, one I get to choose how to assign meaning to: I wanted to stop pretending to make it work with David. And that did it.

I never told David about spending the night with my ex, but I imagine he suspected it. And with the power of hindsight, I can see David would have left anyway. That snowy afternoon when David said, "I love you, but I have to leave," I nodded. It was inevitable but not surprising—a boring end to a narrative we had once believed held so much promise. He kissed me on the forehead. I had that feeling of being outside of my body, watching him talk at me, our breath foggy in the winter air, my inner voice saying, "Thank you for leaving."

My now-voice says, *What the fuck was up with that condescending forehead kiss?* And I wish I had been the one brave enough to come out and ask him to leave. Instead, I said, "What about Tiffany's wedding next week? I RSVP'd for two."

"You're joking," he said, though he could see I wasn't, so he shook his head, saying, "You'll just have to go alone."

"I can't go alone when I've said there will be two of us. The wedding is next week. On Valentine's Day. And it's a formal wedding. Fancy. Everything's set."

"A wedding? I'm leaving, and you're bringing up a fucking wedding?"

I knew he was angry. He never said the word *fucking*, and he didn't like it when I used it, which was often.

"Sorry," I said, even though I was already trying to figure out who to bring in his place. And that's what I was thinking about as he drove off too. Not that I had failed at another relationship. Not that my lover was leaving three weeks into our cohabitation. Not that I would likely never see him again—and still haven't—but that going to my friend Tiffany's wedding alone would screw up her seating arrangements.

Throughout the affair I had learned to compartmentalize things in order to distract myself from thinking about the hard things—I was divorced, had lost my house, my furniture, and many of our mutual friends. The only things I had left were the teaching job I had outgrown, the dog I shared with my ex, and the car I would total on an icy road within a week. I was going into debt renting an overpriced Nevada condo decorated *Miami Vice* style, with white carpets and gold framed mirrors on every wall, including the stairwell.

I went back inside and called my friend Andy to invite him to the wedding. I left a message saying, "Find something fabulous to wear. This wedding is going to be fancy as fuck."

I have never been good at letting go of things, and this relationship was a thing I had wanted so badly, or so I thought. I walked around my rented condo and took down all the pictures of David and put them into a box. I sat on my borrowed couch, and I felt dazed and relieved—what should have been no more than a weeklong fling in Mexico was finally, mercifully, over.

What I needed had been my freedom, an untethered life of wandering the world. I needed these things without having to apologize for needing them. I could now see it was never about David; rather, I had fallen in love with the world—first Mexico and then Spain. I was in love with the soaring cathedrals, the olive trees, and the tapas bars. I was in love with the Plaza Mayor and strong coffee served in delicate china cups on white saucers. I loved the young women navigating the cobblestone streets in their high heels, shopping during siesta, and I loved the old men playing chess in the park.

When I think of David now, it's in that nostalgic way, where the story is full of sensory detail but no plot. I can't remember the smell of his body, only the musty Alhambra or baguettes at a Paris café. I can't remember the sound of his voice, only the birdsong of an early morning in Cuernavaca, the beating heels of a flamenco dancer in Seville, the seals barking in San Sebastian, the chiming of Big Ben with each new hour. I can't remember the taste of his mouth, only the barky depth of a Guinness in a dark Dublin bar, a red wine in the caves of Burgundy, strawberry gelato in Florence. I don't remember our fumbling lovemaking, only the way the damp fog of a Normandy beach curled over the salty horizon, the winking lights of Monaco at midnight, and the shudder of walking among the olive trees, in search of the place where the poet Federico García Lorca had been shot.

Sportfucking

I came home with a bladder infection.

I told my husband I had eaten too many carbohydrates—doughnuts, bagels, croissants, dinner rolls. You know how those writing conferences are: starchy foods for breakfast, lunch, and dinner. And the weather—humidity is bad for female parts! I know I am not fooling you (who doesn't know a lot of sex sometimes leads to bladder infections?), and I only fooled him because there are times when the truth, though obvious as a raindrop, is too hard to accept, even if it has landed on your nose.

And he wasn't my husband. Craig was now my live-in ex-husband, which makes some of this seem better, some of it worse. This live-in ex-husband of mine and I were not exactly having a fairy-tale romance, so when this poet I knew said, "Come see me," I didn't wait around for him to ask twice.

I didn't want the guy to marry me. I just wanted to fuck. When my friend Liv heard about this, she exclaimed with delight, "Sportfucking!" I was happy to have the right term for what I was about to do. The plan to sportfuck all weekend wasn't explicitly stated, but in our emails the poet had made his vasectomy known, and I had made clear my crotch was a no-fly zone unless he submitted to a battery of STD testing beforehand. He complied, and we set a date.

This poet wasn't exactly a hunka burning love. He was (and I assume still is) a wisp of a man, older than me by more than ten years and what you might call very delicate. He had tiny wrists, and the bones of his spine lined his back like pebbles. He was famous enough in the small pond of the poetry world that I won't use his real name. I will call him Werther, not because of any suicidal tendencies but because I wanted to think of him as a Romantic, even though I knew that wasn't anywhere close to the truth.

Months earlier Werther had come to my hometown to give a poetry reading, mostly because we had engaged in some email flirtation, and it seemed exciting—a little thrill to break up the monotony of grading papers, college committee meetings, and a live-in ex-husband. He had come, along with another poet whom I had no interest in fucking. They both read, and afterward, I offered to show them some good old-fashioned hospitality by taking them across the state line into Nevada to the casino dance club, where at midnight all the bikini-clad cage dancers do away with their tops.

My live-in ex-husband wasn't about to let me go off to the dance club alone with two poets and my recently divorced friend, so he came along as well. My friend was, at that time, engaged in what she called "serial dating." Middle-aged but hardly frumpy, she caught the eye of all the fifty-year-olds on Match.com, so she was getting plenty of action, but action begets action, and she, too, was impressed by Werther and his verse, even though she knew I had a crush on him. To be fair to Werther, he was good-looking, in a scholarly kind of way, and smart and fake humble, which tends to go a long way with women.

My recently divorced friend and Werther were grinding up a storm among the twenty-somethings on the dance floor, and I was glad for the moment because I thought this somehow proved to Craig that I, myself, was not at all attracted to the poet. Divorce or no divorce, this was betrayal. We had moved back in together, had agreed to try to make it work.

Soon enough, Craig was satisfied that I wasn't interested in Werther, so he left and went home. By this time my friend and Werther had made out on the dance floor (and, I later learned, in the parking lot too), and he had begged her to come back to his hotel. She was drunk but not drunk enough, so she declined. At that point, I am ashamed to say, I did what any mean girl would do: I swooped in on Werther. After that I have to admit things are a margarita blur. I knew if I didn't go home I would be in big trouble with my live-in ex-husband and even bigger trouble with my recently divorced friend, who had jumped in a taxi home once she saw Werther flirting with me. Werther then begged me to come to his hotel, and I said no, though I promised to visit him later to finish it off.

The next day everything seemed to settle back into place. My live-in ex-husband didn't say a word, my recently divorced friend was angrier at Werther than at me (and probably herself, though in that little triangle I don't think any of us was without guilt), and my hangover was finished by evening. I knew Werther was an opportunist. I was not available, as he had planned, so he went for someone who was. I should also say I had a history of accepting bad behavior from men.

I kept my promise, and a few months later, when Werther picked me up at the airport, he was wearing his usual poet black. He held wilting red roses and a little box of chocolates, which were already melting in the heat. I thought the wilting roses terribly romantic, which made me nervous. Plus, he was a poet with some clout, and I wanted to impress him. But when I'm nervous, I talk. A lot. So I talked the entire trip from the airport, telling Werther one embarrassing thing after the next about myself, until the moment we were almost killed.

We were on a two-lane highway, behind a giant truck. In the opposing lane was another giant truck. I suppose the pickup trying to pass the giant truck in the other lane didn't see us behind the giant truck in our lane. Or didn't care. We couldn't go into the other lane because of giant truck number one, and right then we were traveling across a bridge, so there were no shoulders on either side. With the pickup coming straight for us and nowhere to go, Werther and I both did the only thing we could do: we shut our eyes and screamed. We should have hit the pickup head on. We should have faced a shattering of glass, our organs bungled by steel. We should have been in a terrible accident. But when we opened our eyes, we were past the bridge on the opposite shoulder. Don't ask me how that happened. There are very few incidents in my life for which I can't come up with rational explanations, and this is one of them.

We sat on the side of the dark road and shook with disbelief, fear, relief, and adrenaline. A blizzard in my veins, an icicle for a spine, despite the heat. I am sure we must have said something to one another, something like "Wow" or "Holy shit," but I remember only the shivering and then the driving in silence.

We arrived at Werther's rancher, crossed the lawn, went inside, took off our clothes, and went to bed for two days. This is an exaggeration, of course, but just barely. I remember eating pancakes while Werther read me a horrifying David Foster Wallace story about a child's genitals being badly burned. And a steamy afternoon walk, where I nervously talked and talked, telling Werther I had been to a psychic who told me someone on the other side of the country was thinking about me, and didn't he think it must have been him? And a trip to the university, where Werther had to pick something up from his office. There he introduced me to a woman, and at first glance I knew he was fucking her too.

Other than these small errands, we spent the time in bed. Liv was right: not until that weekend and never after it has fucking felt so much like sport. Werther must have been in his late forties at the time, and I can't imagine he pulled off this feat without some pharmaceutical help, but he denied it. At first I thought this frenzy of fucking was due to the near-accident, the fact that really we ought to have been dead. I figured all we wanted to do was to prove our bodies were still alive, that our hearts were beating, and other things too. That on a hot southern night we had cheated death. Maybe even witnessed a miracle. A God neither of us would claim had saved us. There's the unspeakable—pushing back the presence of God with the pleasures of the body. Or maybe it's the search for God in the moment of sweaty, bodily ecstasy. The ancient religious poems are full of erotic imagery; the ecstatic can only be reached through God or through fucking. Were we in touch with something more spiritual, or was it really just sportfucking? I can turn anything into anything else if I think about it long enough.

One of my favorite plays is Tennessee Williams's *A Streetcar Named Desire*. In it the character Blanche says, "Death . . . is the opposite of desire." I have deeply considered that line, and I'm not sure it's true. Rather, I think that death's proximity intensifies desire. The end of things—the suffering we have endured or are sure to face—intensifies our desires and our wantings.

On our way back to the airport, I tried not to chatter on and on, which wasn't that hard because I was tired. Werther didn't ask to see me again, and I didn't mention seeing him again either. Goodbye was just that.

At the airport I sat on my carry-on at the gate, and I called my recently divorced friend to apologize. She said she didn't care and tried to make me feel better. I think she may have asked why I went to see Werther, what I was looking for. I felt like a balloon that had sailed across the room, spurting air. Once loud and ridiculous, now finally still. Empty and crumpled. The airport is an appropriate place for loneliness. No one makes the pretense of staying. Everyone is going somewhere and usually with great haste.

I ended up giving the sad chocolates Werther had given me to my students to make up for missing a day of class to go to a "writing conference." In my mind the writing conference excuse wasn't an entire lie: I went to spend time with an established poet. Werther carried around his notebook all weekend, at least the few times we left his bed. God only knows what he was writing. Yet being with him made me feel like less of a poet, not more of one. At one point he told me he thought the poet bares the world, and I still don't know if he meant *bares* or *bears*. I was too embarrassed to ask. Maybe he was baring the world while I was bearing it? I didn't write a word that weekend. Later I wrote humiliating, self-indulgent poems.

When I came back from my trip, my sister Cindy said, "It's as if you are in a car and you have pulled your hands off the wheel, ready to crash." Everything at that time in my life was like that. Going to visit Werther was like pressing on the accelerator, closing my eyes, and waiting to crash.

Somehow I had managed a series of near misses.

I didn't—and still don't—care that I was one of many of Werther's women. He wasn't my only affair either. I suppose I went to see Werther because I wanted to have a life that was exciting and free and maybe even reckless—it meant people would like my stories, though when we don't get beyond reckless, there is no point to the story.

I wanted to be more than myself, though now I see how contradictory it all was. What I wanted was to be someone who could take charge of her life, though really, I was doing the opposite. Did I really believe I would look in the mirror and think, *Why, who is that woman who can jet off to the South for a clandestine affair in a 1970s rancher with a man who weighs less than she does?*

That's what I ended up doing, but I suppose what I really wanted was to believe I wasn't the sort of woman who talks too much about silly things when she is nervous. I wanted to be the woman who could go off and fuck someone who cared nothing about her and feel just fine. The truth is, there is no woman like that, and if there was, I am not sure I would admire her. I'm not trying to be moralistic here. I am not saying sex without love is an awful thing because I don't believe that either. I don't regret my sportfucking weekend. Antibiotics took care of the infection, and my live-in ex-husband and I were on our way out anyway.

My friend Kim told me if it isn't true, it's just noise. And here's the truth: I didn't want to have a relationship with Werther. In fact, I wanted to be free to do whatever I wanted. But still, I wanted Werther to like me. But he didn't like me or my sexy middle-aged friend or maybe not even his colleague at the university. What I can see now, after all these years, is that I didn't like him either. I needed an escape from my humiliating living situation. I used Werther, and that didn't make me like myself very much either.

Life is full of all sorts of surprises, though, and a few years later Werther and I ended up in the same plane and then the same taxi on the way to a real writing conference. *Why don't we all share a cab?* my friend Eve suggested. Squeezed in next to him in the back seat of the taxi, the only word that came to mind was *impossible*.

The body remembers things based on feel, based on the temperature of a landscape. I was jogging one morning in Florida, and if you have ever been to Florida in July, you know the prickly stars of a wet heat on your cheeks, the stinging fire in your lungs. The body's machine working against the heat. I ran, and I remembered that walk through a late-afternoon glare, how I had talked about "my psychic," and how that must have sounded. How I let my sweaty hand dangle next to his, hoping. It all comes back, whether I like it or not: the near-accident on the highway, the football announcer's tinny voice coming from the cracking loudspeakers at the nearby stadium, the dead lawn, the afternoon heat seeping through the blinds, the weight of my suitcase.

This Far from Desire

One of the reasons I had cited to Craig for our divorce was our differing worldviews. I told him I wanted nothing more than to travel the world.

"We went to Mexico on our honeymoon," he said.

"Exactly," I said. "We went to an all-inclusive resort in Ixtapa."

"So?"

"I want to do more," I had said. "That's not really traveling." And with that I started planning a seven-week trip to Central America to study Spanish. Alone. I booked at two different language schools, where I would stay with local families in order to have the full language immersion. I told Craig I needed to do this to become fluent in Spanish for my doctoral work, which was true. But the truer truth was I wanted to escape. Craig and I had broken up, and after we had both had various affairs and the divorce was final, we did the next logical thing—we moved back in together.

But it wasn't working, so I booked a flight to Guatemala and left for my summer break.

At a weaving cooperative outside of Antigua, I watched as a young woman knelt on the cracked earth, braiding fabric—red and black figures on green, the shapes of flowers and birds. Her callused fingers re-created the sky. She told me she sold her first *huipil* at five. Her toes bent beneath her, the balls of her feet white like garlic bulbs. A baby slept in the sling on her

back. I asked her how old she was. She answered, "Dieciocho."
Eighteen.

She asked me how many children I had.

"No tengo ninguno." I have none.

She wrinkled her forehead and said, "Todavía no." Not yet.

I told her I was old enough to be her mother, and she laughed,
went back to her weaving, showing me what each color stood
for: yellow is for corn, blue for the sea; red symbolized blood,
and black was for the war. "Siempre," she said. Always the war.
She looked up from her weaving and said, "Green is reality."

I set off for a hike, passing poinsettias, stray chickens and
dogs, through the mud—it was the rainy season. Children came
running after me, begging. Their toes curled over the rocks in
the trail. I paid them three *quetzales* for their photograph. I
met a local woman on the trail and asked her about the cloth
draped on her head. She told me it meant she was married.
The unmarried women wear the cloth on their shoulder, to
show they are not taken. She said it used to be that a man who
was interested would pull the cloth from the shoulder of the
unmarried woman, and that meant he wanted a date. This could
cause problems for the woman because if she thought him *viejo
y feo*—old and ugly—he could still force the date. The parents
would talk it over. The woman's opinion didn't matter.

A small waterfall weaved down the green hillside. Puddles
formed in the mud. I asked if it was still like that. "Not anymore," she said and then added, "well, not always."

"But that's not fair," I said. She smiled and said she didn't
think so either. The girl, she said, should get to choose.

Craig had told me he didn't need to do any more traveling
than to stay at a resort, so when he emailed to tell me he had
bought a plane ticket to meet me in Guatemala, I was surprised.
I told myself I should be happy he had listened to me, that he

was trying. I wondered if maybe I hadn't tried hard enough. I believed that because I had been the one who had been caught cheating (Craig read my journal) and asked for the divorce—it was my fault. And if I could break it, maybe I could fix it? I took the try-try-try-again maxim to the limit.

As Craig's arrival approached, I began to think of this as our "save-the-marriage trip," even though the divorce had been final for months and the marriage had been over long before that, both logistically and emotionally.

Yet if we could travel together, I reasoned, we could be happy together again.

My last week alone in Guatemala, I drifted around Antigua, a town so beautiful it seemed like a dream, wondering what would happen when Craig arrived. I walked circles through the cobbled streets, following women wearing baby slings and carrying jugs on their heads. Buses decorated with wild airbrushed paintings honked, the church bells rang, horse hooves on stone echoed, and ravens screeched overhead. An ice cream vendor jingled his bells and yelled "helado, helado, helaaaadoooo" under the shade of the *llama de bosque*; the tree's beauty matched its name: *flame of the forest*. A shoe shiner watched everyone's feet as they passed, hoping for a customer. A group of schoolchildren settled into benches, wearing paper crowns and eating Happy Meals. The fountain in the town plaza bubbled, and at night the twinkly lights in the plaza reflected off the rain-soaked streets.

I surprised Craig by meeting him at the airport. Craig had never traveled alone, and he didn't speak Spanish, so I couldn't imagine him arriving in Guatemala City, trying to find his way to Antigua. When he saw me at the gate, he seemed relieved. Maybe he had thought this trip would save us, too, and seeing me there was a sign?

In the taxi I chatted to him about all the things I'd planned for us to do. The next day was market day in Chichicastenango.

"Won't that be fun?" I asked. I thought the busier we kept, the better. At the time I didn't see this for what it was: a distraction from each other.

We arrived at my homestay, and the family had moved me from the attic room with a twin bed to a bedroom on the main floor with a *cama matrimonial*. I had told them *mi esposo* was coming. My husband. It was close enough to the truth that was impossible to explain, at least in my limited Spanish.

"Do you want to nap?" I asked Craig when we arrived. He pulled me toward him. A painting of the Virgin Mary with doleful eyes stared down at us from beneath a gold frame. Her white hands folded across her chest like wings.

"Not here," I said in a whisper.

"Why not?" he asked.

"Because of the family. They'll hear us."

"So what? We're married," he said. "It's okay."

"But we aren't really." I pulled away.

"They don't know that."

I stood up, shook my head, and said, "Sleep if you're tired. If not, let's go to the plaza and walk around. I'm hungry anyway. Don't you want to see Antigua?"

He said he could use a nap, and I went out alone, looking for something to eat.

The man who had pulled us aboard the Chichicastenango-bound bus stood in the open door, whistling to other cars and buses, letting them know we were passing. The music blasted, and every time the bus stopped, people bustled to get out, and the man in the doorway climbed onto the top of the bus and threw down packages. I sat in one of the aisle seats, squished between two people, so my butt cheeks weren't on a seat but suspended in midair; we were packed in so tightly, I hardly moved, despite the looping curves along the canyon road. A television hanging from the ceiling played a show on grizzlies in Alaska, a world away. The Radiohead song "Creep" blasted from the speakers. I loved the bus and the music, the strange juxtaposition of the grizzly video and the crowd—meanwhile, Craig stood near me sweating; he clutched to the silver rail so tightly his whole fist went as white as a dead fish.

When we got to the market, Craig said, "Okay. I did the chicken bus. Once is enough."

"You didn't think it was fun?" I asked, but I already knew the answer. I was right back to being passive-aggressive with him. My better self, the version of who I became when I traveled, was already gone.

One of the things Craig and I loved to do together was hike, so the next day I suggested a guided trip up Volcano Pacaya. Craig didn't think we needed a guide.

"It's not to help us find the way," I said. "It's to protect us."

"From what?" Craig asked.

"Banditos."

He laughed. "You and your imagination."

Because I could speak Spanish and he couldn't, I arranged the trip and hired a guide who carried a big machete. On the trail we passed a group of men, their faces concealed by bandanas, their hands gripping machetes. Our guide greeted them as we passed. I told Craig you either paid for the guide or you paid the bandits. Hiring the guide was far easier and less scary. Craig still didn't believe me. And who knows? Maybe he had been right. Craig had the uncanny ability to make me doubt myself.

We hiked through a steady rain, along a narrow path through the jungle and then up the spine of the volcano; at the crest we reached the black volcanic rock. We summited another ridge, and the earth below our feet let off white steam. At one point we were enveloped in a cloud of sulfur, and the fumes choked us. I didn't want to go any further, but I knew Craig would be disappointed if we turned back.

Then the wind blew, and the cloud disappeared, showing glimpses of the rocky top. Smoke seeped from the earth, the lava glowed orange and red between the black rock, fire and molten rocks spurted from the crater. The earth rumbled, sounding as if it were heaving breaths. I was standing at the trapdoor to the world's hot center. Never before had I been so convinced the earth is a living thing.

We stood at the edge, and the guide told us to be careful, that the rocks shooting out were thousands of degrees hot. In the United States there would be ropes and signs and rules. Here we could get as close as our folly permitted. One group of tourists climbed the rocks above the crater. A plume of smoke rose, obscuring them. I backed away from the volcano's mouth; the smoke cleared, and I squinted into the hot crater, feeling the urge of vertigo—the pull of gravity that makes me want to leap. I stepped back from the edge.

Rather than taking the trail, we jogged down the side of the volcano, the rubble slowing each step, so we didn't pitch forward. We laughed together as we loped down the volcanic scree. Night fell, and we hiked the rest of the way through the jungle in the dark, following our guide and the yellow light of our headlamps. I was wet and cold but felt slightly outside of my shivering body. I was happy enough to think that maybe the "save-the-marriage" trip really was working, even if we were no longer married. I didn't even point out to Craig that without the guide, we would have never found our way home in the dark.

That night at a restaurant in Antigua, the service was slow, so we sat across from each other, trying to come up with things to talk about, which should have been easy since we had seen and done so much over the past few days. Instead, we argued about the Spanish word for "candle." Craig said it was *la candela*, and I argued it was *la vela*. When our waiter finally arrived, we ordered wine, which tasted terrible, and it felt good to agree about something.

Over the next few days, I rattled off a list of reasons to Craig about why I couldn't have sex with him: toothache, canker sores, too many mosquitoes, stomachache, pimples on my chin. When we arrived at La Casa del Mundo in Lago de Atitlán and checked into our red tile–floored room with French doors that opened onto a patio overlooking the lake and volcano behind it, I had run out of excuses and realized it would be easier to say yes than no.

Afterward I wrote in my journal: "It was fine but not fabulous."

And that's the best I can do because I have no memory of the sex. Sometimes I imagine powerful goodbye sex, complete with tears; but most times I picture a woman staring at the whitewashed ceiling with its rustic wooden beams, wishing she had been left alone.

The trip didn't reignite our marriage, but it did something more important. The sex between us had always been good—a glitter glue holding us together. Now even that was gone. I also wrote this into my journal: *How is it that we have come this far from desire?* Fine but not fabulous meant neither; it meant forgettable; it meant the marriage was finally over. And I realized the loss of my marriage, but also the old ideas I held about myself and the way my life should unfold, was necessary in order to gain the freedom and self-knowledge I had always been seeking.

And as it turns out, there are always two ways of saying things, of seeing the world. Both *la vela* and *la candela* mean "candle."

Traveling Alone

Maybe it was the drinks on empty stomachs or the dimly lit Quito bar or my exuberant dance floor fan kick that encouraged my young companions to forget I was nearly twice their age. Liam and Adam sandwiched me into what can only be called a grind, and I thought about the beautiful star of *Y Tu Mamá También*, the movie in which the much older but totally gorgeous woman, played by Maribel Verdú, has a threesome with two much younger men. Boys, really. And that's how it felt—like I was Maribel Verdú and Adam and Liam were the two seventeen-year-old boys in the film.

Liam and Adam were in their early twenties, and I was thirty-six, so we were all older than the characters, and not a one of us nearly as beautiful, but the age difference had to be about the same. But that's what a movie in your head does—it morphs time and reason. In other words, whenever I feel like I am watching my life as if it were a movie, I'm totally fucked, or at least about to be, figuratively or literally. But I wasn't thinking that, not at the time; rather, this thought crept into my mind: *Wasn't a threesome something I wanted to cross off my bucket list of transgressions?*

I had recently divorced and was traveling alone in South America. I was leaving Ecuador for Peru the next day, and Liam and Adam were headed to Bolivia. I was protected by the anonymity of travel, and I would surely never see them again. Wasn't part of the allure of travel to leave your old self behind and embrace a more adventurous, interesting, reckless self? I was in my midthirties, young enough to think I could be anyone I wanted to be, old enough to know I would always, somehow, settle back into the me I had always been, whether I was hiking the Andes or at home on the couch, grading student papers. I knew being a new person because of a new place was impossible, but that didn't stop me from fantasizing.

I had met Liam and Adam earlier that day on one of those tours that promised "authentic" experiences and visits to local markets. And my naïveté left me unprepared for what followed. I had thought this day trip from Quito would be a good way to meet other people. These two young Englishmen were taking a gap year between university and everything else. Adam was a heavyset fellow with a swoop of auburn hair, and Liam was a slip of a thing with a lisp. They told me they were two weeks into a yearlong trip, though Adam already missed his girlfriend at home. "Stop talking about her already, would you?" Liam told him.

Liam might have been small, but he was bossy. If I were making bets, I didn't think those two would last more than a month into their travels.

Our small tour group rode in the van together, and when the Soft Cell version of "Tainted Love" came on the radio, we all sang along. Our group also included a Dutch woman named Natalie, an Israeli tour guide, and Mario, our Ecuadorian driver-translator. I thought about the ways music crossed all nationalities and languages—here we were, American, Dutch, British, Israeli, and Ecuadorian, singing the words to this 1980s hit. The rugged greenscape of the Ecuadorian mountains laddered the gray sky. A man herded black-and-white-spotted cows. A pig and a German shepherd were chained to a fence.

Our first stop was at a "real" shepherd's home, a mud-thatched house shaped like a beehive with a hole at the top for cooking smoke to escape. The blackened walls and dirt floors made the hut seem darker. Liam said, "My God" when he looked inside, and I hoped the shepherd didn't speak English, but just in case he did, I said he had a very nice house. Although I was living in an eight-hundred-square-foot A-frame cabin at the time, a house I sometimes called "a hovel," it was like a mansion compared to this earthen-made hut on the side of a windswept mountain.

The shepherd and his house had become a tourist attraction. He needed the money, so he stood and posed while tourists took photographs of them, no doubt posting them on Facebook and boasting about visiting a "real shepherd's home." Certainly, this was staged for the tourists, but still, it left me feeling uncomfortable.

The shepherd grinned, showing the missing teeth. He pointed out his *cuy*, and Mario translated from Quechua, the language of the Andes, to Spanish. The Israeli tour guide then translated the Spanish into English: "He is showing us his guinea pigs," as if that wasn't already obvious. Squeals came from a cage in the corner. It was not only commonplace to find live guinea pigs in restaurant kitchens, but many people kept caged guinea pigs in their own kitchens, a delicacy for special occasions. Natalie said, "I could never eat a guinea pig!"

We thanked the shepherd and moved onto our next destination: market day in Sasquili, which meant the streets filled with everything from fruit and vegetables to live animals, including more *cuy*. Men worked on sewing machines, tailoring clothes for customers, who were waiting and gossiping with their friends from neighboring towns. A woman stood by with a basket of rabbits and chickens. A potential customer came by, felt the bodies under the white feathers. While the women negotiated a fair price, the customer ruffled her fingers along the bellies. Hanging upside down, the chickens did nothing, resigned, it seemed, to their own deaths.

Women sorted through beans and rabbits, socks and eye shadow. A man whipped yelping hogs with a stick to load them into a pickup truck. A lamb tied to the top of a bus bleated in terror. We all took pictures, and I wrote notes in my journal. Novel to me but quotidian to the locals—ordinary is a matter of perspective. And then Natalie said, "I can't take this. All these live animals. I'm an animal lover. I want to go."

We started back to the van, and a young woman walked toward us and lifted her blouse, revealing a gash, red as a plum, where a nipple should be. She held out her hand and mouthed the word "Ayúdame." *Help me.* Her face in a squint. We hurried past, looked down at the dirt road. I looked back, and so did she. She turned and started walking back toward me. I scrambled to find change in my pocket, placed it into the nest of her palm, knowing there was nothing my coins could do for her. We left the woman and walked away; Natalie didn't say a word, and neither did I.

The cliffside restaurant where we ate lunch perched at the edge of Quilotoa, an extinct volcano. Far below sat a small sapphire lake in the crater's center. Natalie, the Dutch girl who loved animals, ordered lamb, and I tried to smile at Liam and Adam, but they didn't notice. Weren't we all beings of contradiction in some way or another?

When our food came, I watched Natalie saw at her meat with a dull knife. She told us it was her birthday and asked if we would join her for a drink later that night. We all agreed.

After lunch we hiked down a steep, sandy path into the throat of the extinct volcano. A local boy followed us down and then asked us if we wanted to buy a ride back up on his mule. We declined, and the boy looked disappointed. When I realized I might have made his day or even his week with my ride, I paid him a small tip to take a photograph together at the lip of the crater.

Our little tour group then boarded the van and drove back to Quito. There was no chatter, the usual where-are-you-from and where-are-you-going and where-have-you-been of travelspeak. But when ABBA's "Gimme! Gimme! Gimme! (A Man after Midnight)" came on the radio, we all sang along.

In the Quito dance club of Natalie's choosing, she said she liked to drink but wasn't so keen on dancing. Because I am fond of both drinking and dancing, perhaps overly so, I skipped onto the dance floor. By the second or third song, Adam was behind me, his face over my shoulder, nuzzling his chin into my collarbone. Liam took a position in front of me and placed both hands on my waist, while Adam attempted to spark a fire between his nether regions and my ass. This is where I started to wonder if there might be a threesome in my future, where the movie reel played in my head, looking like someone else's life. Certainly, for Adam and Liam, this was just dancing, and the lusty story line belonged to me alone.

And what was wrong with me anyway? I had seen real suffering—the woman with the gash in her breast, even the lamb tied to the top of the bus—and here I was thinking about a threesome with two much-too-young men?

Before I could find out what was really happening on that dance floor, I slipped out from between them, ghosting my new friends. I walked out of the club and into the cold night air alone. Taxis honked and flashed their lights at me, wondering if I wanted a ride. I shook my head, waved them away, and walked the few blocks back to my hostel. And maybe that's the thing about travel; it enables us to get outside of ourselves, to try on new stories, to take paths we wouldn't otherwise follow.

I fell into the narrow bed in my bare hostel room. I wondered if the movie in my head really would follow the script of *Y Tu Mamá También* in real life. If so, those two boys would be making out with each other in their own hostel bedroom soon.

And I would die very young.

But the thing, of course, was that I was no longer very young.

Winter Travel

There is no wilderness quite like traveling through a blizzard at night. Snow blew a frozen web across my windshield, the red brake lights in front of me appearing and disappearing with wind gusts. Snowflakes shined white in the headlights, leaving everything else in the globed dark. Highway 50 was closed for avalanche blasting, gusting snow, and poor visibility—I could delay returning home one more day. I was always happier wearing travel's cloak of anonymity, but also I could put off telling my ex-husband it was finally over.

The innkeeper at the lodge told me I could have a room without a bathroom for thirty dollars and handed me a flashlight. A fallen lodgepole pine had smashed the power lines—no lights, no heat, no phones. The innkeeper looked like Norman Bates dressed as his mother. She told me, "We have no electricity and no food, but the bar is open."

I read Gabriel García Márquez with a flashlight, ate pretzels, and drank Zinfandel at the candlelit bar. The men who wear yellow plastic suits, put tire chains on and off, were in the bar— with the road closed, the visibility zero, the cars stranded on the highway, no one needed their chains put on, so they were without work. The man sitting next to me looked about my age, midthirties, or maybe a few years younger. He wore his long brown hair in dreadlocks. Even though I've never liked the appropriation of dreadlocks by white people, I found myself wanting to touch the tangled columns of hair.

I took another sip of wine, went back to Fermina Daza and Florentino Ariza's unlikely romance. And I eavesdropped, taking notes in my journal. The dreadlocks man turned to me, asked, "What are you writing?" I lied, said I was writing about my recent trip to Latin America. I couldn't tell him I was writing about him. Or could I?

He asked, "What are people there like?"

"They are the same as here," I said, "but better."

He smiled wide, showing black rectangles of missing teeth at the back of his mouth. A gold ring circled each hazel iris of his eyes. Grease gathered underneath the fingernails. Motorists—colleagues from the college where I teach—would call him *Chain Monkey*. From my eavesdropping I learned he lived across the highway in a camper, would have steak the inn had given him for supper. I did not learn his name. I could smell his body under the yellow snowsuit. We had nothing more to say to one another. I went back to my journal, wrote about how I could follow him across the road, drifts of snow collapsing under each step. Then the yellow vinyl peeling from skin, the snow pelting the metal shell of the camper—that story. That transgression and the familiar loneliness that inevitably follows.

An affair to erase the other affairs. And no one would ever find out. Judy Collins sang about doing this with her own dark-haired stranger in "The Blizzard," clarifying her decision to leave.

But it would be years before I heard that old song, and I didn't want to be with him; I just needed to try on the idea. What I wanted was to sit at the dark bar with my glass of red wine and my book. I wanted to walk up the creaky stairs to a room with a narrow bed and watch giant flakes of snow through a window. I didn't need to hear birdsong or frogs or the music of a foreign tongue—the things I believed I needed to escape.

The man in the yellow suit finished his beer, waved to me, and pulled his hood over his head. He left the bar with a gush of cold air as the door opened and closed.

The storm blew out overnight, leaving a crystallized blue day, a sparkling snowscape. I drove up Highway 50, past the snow-coated trees, their graceful white branches like the arms of dancing brides. I passed Horsetail Falls, the craggy Lover's Leap, and Ralston Peak. Electric wires sagged over the highway, coated with snow and ice; the green elevation sign read 7,382 feet at the top of Echo Summit.

I followed the frozen ribbon of road, through the constellation of white-sequined trees under the vaulted blue sky. The first sight of Lake Tahoe from the top of the pass snagged at my breath, the way it does for so many tourists who see the lake for the first time. I couldn't help from feeling like an outsider in my own life—that loneliness.

At the same time, I was home. And looking out over the dark-blue lake and ever-shifting mountainscape, I settled into my aloneness, accepting the wild heart's fantasies while knowing that desire itself—the wanting but never having—is sometimes enough.

The Hungry Bride

"You'd better go on a warpath," Liv told me, "or in a month you'll hate yourself." I had called my friend Liv because I had looked at my calendar and realized I was exactly one month out to my wedding, my second wedding, and at thirty-nine I couldn't do anything about being an older bride, but I figured I might be able to do something about being a chubby one. I had bought the form-fitting dress, had hired an expensive photographer, and like any bride, I wanted to look good for the pictures. I could hear my mother saying, "The camera adds ten pounds. Maybe fifteen."

At the moment, I had a chin and a half and a pooch belly. I had bought one of those bridal magazines so thick it could double as doorstop or a weapon. All the brides were thin, which we have been conditioned to believe is the same thing as elegant. Against my own better judgment, I called Liv for advice; she had suffered with anorexia and had dieted into a size double zero—whatever that was—for her own wedding.

"Write everything down, everything. Even gum. Don't go over 1,300 calories. And work out every day for an hour. Do sprints. You can lose eight, maybe ten, before the wedding."

"I can't believe I'm calling you for dieting advice. Seems like really bad form."

"No. I'm really good at this. I can help. This is my specialty."

I hung up and began by writing everything down. It was amazing how fast I could get to 1,300 calories. I could get there before 9:00 a.m., and I usually do most of my eating after 9:00 p.m. I decided to figure out what was in 1,300 calories and eat the exact same thing every day so I wouldn't have to keep googling calorie content.

This tactic worked until I had a party to go to. I lied to the hostess, telling her I had already eaten, and I did my best not to stand near the appetizer table.

The hostess asked, "How about dessert?"

I shook my head.

"Just have one brownie. It's a little one," she said. I declined, and she practically chased me around the house with that damn brownie—skinny bitch was probably trying to burn off her own calories, I thought as she stalked me. In the end she wrapped it up and sent it home with me. Also, everyone else offered me wine again and again. I love wine, but at 150 calories, I would rather have a bowl of light popcorn. Or two hard-boiled eggs. Or a giant salad with light dressing. It didn't take long to memorize the numbers and add it up in my head.

I got home and called Liv. "Everyone wanted me to eat and drink," I said.

"That happens. Tell them you're getting married. Everyone will leave you alone. People get that."

"I did. They still wanted me to eat brownies and drink wine."

"But you didn't, did you?"

"Nope."

"Good."

The truth is if I had started, I wouldn't have been able to stop. The best thing was to stick with my preplanned menus, which I had to admit wasn't very fun, but it was working. After about ten days I stepped on the scale and had lost five pounds. But that was also about the time I started to get grumpy. And I started dreaming I binged and then would wake up relieved when I realized I was hungry. But after these dreams I felt on edge, snapping at the girl at Starbucks in the morning when she asked, "Can I wrap up a pastry to go with your skinny latte?"

A few days later I was throwing a birthday party for a girl-friend and realized I needed a dessert. I should have gone for a rum-filled fruitcake or something with shaved coconut—things I hate. But cupcakes were on sale at Safeway. *You have control,* I told myself. *You don't have to eat one. They're not for you but for your guests.* When I got to the checkout, all I could do was watch my cupcakes with longing as they traveled the conveyor belt to the checker.

"These are so good. YUM," the checker said when he got to the cupcakes. "I LOVE cupcakes."

"They aren't for me," I said. "I'm having a party. It's my friend's birthday. They are for her."

"But they aren't all for her. You get one. Or two." He smiled.

"No, I don't. I don't get one. Or two. I'm not eating any."

"Why not? These are delicious." He held them above the plastic shopping bag. "I couldn't help myself. I would eat two. Or three. They aren't that big."

"Just put them in the bag, all right, and ring me up." I must have sounded a little frantic, must have scared him, because he dropped my box of cupcakes as if it were a piece of burning coal, and the cupcakes dumped over and got all squished together.

"Sorry, ma'am," he said. "You can go get another box."

"No, it's fine."

"Really, go get another one," the people behind me in line said. "You don't want smashed cupcakes."

But I did want smashed cupcakes. They didn't look as good with the frosting smeared on the top of the box. Maybe then I would be less likely to eat them. "No really, I'm fine," I said. "My friends can eat smashed cupcakes. What do I care?" Then out of a meanness fueled by hunger, I said to the cashier, "You really should be more careful."

The checker looked like he might cry, and I realized that's what my diet was doing to me: I was now the bitch who made grocery store clerks cry. I didn't know what else to say, so I paid and left with my smashed cupcakes.

At the dinner party I reasoned I had been so good, I *deserved* champagne. And after that I deserved white wine. Then red. And at that point two cupcakes didn't sound wholly unreasonable.

When I woke up the next morning, I had a hangover, but worse, I felt cupcake guilt. I vowed to be good for the next three weeks. At the rate I was going, I could lose the fifteen pounds I had gained over the past two years. I could be like those svelte brides in the wedding magazines if only I could control myself.

The magazine really was a weapon.

I wrote down every calorie in a pretty little journal I bought for the purpose. I went back to my 1,300-calorie plan. I became grumpy again. I decided to cheer myself up by buying a few odds and ends at the local Ross Dress for Less. In my small mountain town there are two choices for clothes shopping—Kmart and Ross. This is not an exaggeration. I chose Ross, and I waited in line to check out, trying to ignore my grumbling stomach. I was too busy thinking about how I would have liked a slice of pizza, so I couldn't keep up with the ways the line merged into the one cashier's open register, and a couple with a newborn cut me off. "Hey, you cut," I said, trying to weave my cart back to my position in front of them.

"You weren't paying attention, so it's your fault," the young father said. The mother smirked at me, and even though she held a carrier with a very young human in it, I wanted to hit her.

"You're rude," I said. "You knew I was waiting, and you cut me off."

"You should pay attention next time," the man said. At this point I realized everyone in the line, including the cashier, was staring at us, waiting to see what would happen next. I wanted to call him something other than what I called him, which was "meanie," but I worked at the local community college, and one of my students happened to work at the Ross (luckily, she was stuck back at the changing rooms, counting items, so she missed the show), but I didn't think it should get out that Professor Roberts got into a fistfight with a couple with an infant. That sort of thing doesn't bode well for tenure reviews. I backed down, muttering under my breath about how rude everyone was, but mostly I was mad at myself for getting so hungry, I believed physical violence seemed like a viable option.

Because he is a very smart man, Tom, my husband-to-be, took off on a solo backpacking trip during this time, which is what I should have been doing rather than starving myself. As it turned out, I wasn't invited on my fiancé's mancation, so I planned a trip of my own to visit friends. I warned them I was on a diet, telling them how grumpy I had become as a result. "I'm not eating bad carbohydrates or fried food. And I'm not drinking," I'd said.

"You're not drinking at all?" my friend Andy, who happens to work for a winery, asked.

"Well, not very much," I said.

Andy had a healthy dinner of fish and vegetables waiting for me when I arrived at his house, and I stuck to one glass of wine. I went over a little on the calories but not much. As the days wore on, I got looser and looser with my diet, and by the last night of our visit, I was eating M&M trail mix paired with a petite Syrah. "It's a healthy snack," Andy said as he poured more trail mix into my bowl, more wine in my glass.

At the beginning I had thought dieting wasn't so hard. You eat a controlled amount and make time to exercise. I thought, why, anyone can do it! Even me. However, I soon realized why dieting had become a thirty-five-billion-dollar industry. In theory it's easy to control what goes in your mouth. But it's a slippery slope. The story I told myself constantly changed. One hour I wanted to be thin at any cost; I would do whatever it took. The next hour I reasoned my fiancé loved me exactly as I was and that I couldn't lose too much weight because I didn't have the money for a new wardrobe.

When I returned from my trip, I weighed in and saw I had gained back two of the five pounds and went back, as Liv called it, on the warpath. I had two weeks left. I called another girl-friend, the ever-practical Brenda, for advice.

"Buy a girdle and don't worry about it," she said.

I went online and ordered the SPANX, which promised to smooth out the lumps and bulges. When it came in the mail, I tried it on. It was like biking shorts but made out of a thick support hose material. It pulled me in but didn't do anything for the second chin, so I vowed to stay on the diet until the day of my wedding. I spent my last single days writing down everything I put in my mouth. I planned my meals out for the entire day to the exact calorie (Liv warned me not to go under or my body would shut down). If anything came up, a party or a lunch meet-ing, I panicked. It's almost impossible to count calories in restau-rants. How many calories are in that salad dressing? Who knows.

Even though my wedding diet only lasted a month, I could see how so many girls and women progress to eating disorders. Anything can become habitual. How do you stop counting calories in your head when you have been doing it for so long? It's like any obsession—it controls your brain, takes over your rational mind. Like planning a wedding, but that's finite. The planning ends with the wedding day. In my short dieting tenure, I could see how people get addicted to the loop—basing your worth on the number of calories that go into your mouth is easier, less vulnerable, than tallying acts of kindness or instances of compassion.

Three weeks in, I stepped on the scale again and had lost seven pounds. One week to go, and it was looking like Liv was right—I'd lose eight to ten. She really was an expert. I decided to try the SPANX on with the dress and see how things were shaping up. I pulled on the girdle and then the dress, which was noticeably looser. In the boobs. The dress was a halter with a low back, so I couldn't wear a bra with it—even the bra specialist at Macy's had declared that the dress had to be worn "braless."

Before my crash diet, my breasts filled out the top and held up the dress. Now when I tried it on, I realized I had lost exactly 3.5 pounds per boob. The material puckered, and if I leaned certain ways, the space between the dress and boob was enough to show nipple. Meanwhile, the stomach fit the exact same way, maybe even tighter because my breasts no longer pulled the material up and away from the middle.

I texted Liv: *Disaster. The dress is too loose in the boobs. Must eat.*
She texted me back: *No! Get jelly boobs to put in bra.*
I answered: *Can't wear a bra. Jelly doughnuts not jelly boobs.*

The thing is, I had gotten so used to writing everything down and staying away from my "bad" list—flour, sugar, fried foods, wine—that it was hard going back.

And the truth was, it was easier wasting brain space and time with the diet. That way I didn't have to think so much about what I was about to do and how my new marriage would change my life. About how I would live with someone after living alone for so many years. About how my previous marriage had failed and maybe I really wasn't "the marrying kind" as Andy had once suggested. No—I didn't have to worry about any of that because I was too busy looking up the number of calories in a pear.

The realization that the dress looked better before the diet was a relief—skinny isn't always better. I began getting my boobs back one cupcake at a time. I told my sister Cindy, and she said she had just read about the practice of fattening up girls for marriage in West Africa because a skinny girl has no chance of getting a husband. I suppose it's all how you look at a thing. No one is going to tell you that in an American bridal magazine. No one is going to say, "You'd better plump up to fill out a designer dress." Although certainly both extremes—starvation diets or force-feeding girls to make them look more womanly—speak to unreasonable and unhealthy expectations of beauty for girls and women.

The cupcakes (and maybe a little champagne too) did the trick, and on my wedding day I filled out the dress, and I didn't care if I wasn't thin. What mattered to me was that I was surrounded by my favorite people, and I was marrying the right man this time around. Tom had known enough to keep his mouth shut during the mad monthlong prewedding diet and dealt with his hungry bride with kindness and grace—and also, he knew when to get the hell out of town.

Breaking the Codes

I am there, in the bathroom next door to you, giving my boy-friend head. I'm doing it because that isn't going all the way, so I might not be called a slut at school. I'm not doing it because I like it. This is understood. I'm doing it because he likes it, and what he wants is more important than what I want. I don't look at it that way, though. I just see beige: the walls, the plush carpet, the sink, the towels. It is 1985. Beige is in.

After he is done / I am done, I get off my knees, stumble into the bedroom. You are there, wrapped in a beige blanket. Naked otherwise. The other boys—because they are technically boys even though they are three years older than us—are in a rush to leave. My boyfriend barely rights his clothes, and he is out the door with them. Suddenly everything is very quiet. I remember you are crying. I do not remember what you say to me. It is "we got together" or possibly "they all took me." I don't know; I just know what happened. Sex with more than one of these boys—nearly men—maybe with them all. We hadn't yet learned to say the word *rape*.

"Don't tell anyone," you say—this I am sure of. And I don't tell anyone. Hadn't I invited them over? Wasn't it my fault? We are fourteen.

Now I am forty-seven, and I tell my husband because a man just a few years older than me is about to be confirmed as a Supreme Court judge. Women about my age have come forward, accusing him of the same thing—my secret. But it doesn't seem to matter, this sexual assault. I cry, telling Tom how I invited the boys that long-ago night. I am to blame. He is looking at me, incredulous—this woman who knows better than to blame herself. But the fourteen-year-old girl is still inside this middle-aged body. She still thinks it's her fault. I keep trying to play the reels, and they are the same every time. The apartment in Ventura. Coors Light. Bartles & Jaymes Fuzzy Navel. Drinking games at the table. The bathroom. Finding you. The boys leaving very quickly. Nobody ever saying anything. I want to make sense of this memory— this thing that for so long I have tried to convince myself I didn't really see. But I cannot unsee it even if I don't fully understand it.

If I'd told, we would've both gotten in trouble. We were staying in your dad's apartment when he was out of town. I invited my boyfriend, his friends. We were drinking. Breaking the rules. So I said nothing. To protect you and to protect myself. But the boys, they were my fault.

When my mother died last year, I found all my letters from 1985. Teachers sometimes confiscated our notes, so we wrote in code: WBS, LLL, SSS&S, BFF. *Write back soon, longer letter later, sorry so sloppy and short, best friends forever.* I am surprised these codes come so easily to me even now, more than thirty years later. They're etched into me.

In our letters we say we try to let boys down easy. "It's nothing personal," we learn to say. "We value your friendship." We do not want to hurt them. In other letters I tell my friends—they are girls of thirteen and fourteen—to jump on the boys they like.

What do I mean? We are bodies in perpetual motion too. We just don't know how to own these bodies we inhabit.

Before the older boyfriend in the bathroom, I go with another boy. That's what we call it: "go with." My mother asks me where

I am going, and I am so annoyed with her. She knows. She wants me to see how ridiculous I am, but I'm not ready to see it.

One of the places I go is to see the movie *Footloose*. But really, I never see the movie. I sit in the back row with a boy who fingers me. I don't yet know this should be for my pleasure, but it isn't. He hurts me, and I feel dirty from the inside out. When my father comes to pick us up, he asks how the movie was. I am dazed. I don't know. I must have said something like "So-so." I am thirteen.

But I want to get back to the beige room. I look for clues in your letters. They say things like "I am in auto safety, and Mr. Lochner is playing classical music. This isn't supposed to be a fucking symphony." Your letters say, "I feel so fucking old." Your letters say, "When he comes, I will see what comes up. Bad choice of words. Better get going. The bell's about to ring." Only thirty years later do I get the pun.

In another letter a friend writes to me, "Are you grounded? You must be. I could hear your dad screaming at you over the phone. It scared me." We thought everything was our fault. But Daddy knew his screaming was his, so I was never grounded. Not once. This is what it was like to live with someone screaming Bourbon-fueled tirades at night but self-aware and kind in the morning. He did the best he could. And he always liked you—he said you were so smart. He was right.

I know I am lucky. Drinking and screaming are easy things compared to what you endure.

More letters. Folded origami letters. Letters in code. Letters about hard-ons during sex education (even then we wondered why these films were screened to coed audiences). Letters that apologized for "being dumb," for "being boring," for "being fat," for taking up space. Letters that wondered what "kind of guy" they were. What "kind of girl" they were. What kind of girls *we* were. Letters that saved us. Letters that failed to save us.

You write: "He is telling me he loves me. Don't you think he is pressuring me to tell him I love him? What can I say? He'll call me a bitch. I need one of your stupid lectures."

Another letter tells me our friend's stepdad won't let her boyfriend into the house because he is Black. She tells me she loves him but says she's scared, like, "really, really, really scared." She says her new stepdad wants to control her and her sisters and her mother too. She writes "Private and confidential" on the envelope. She tells me not to tell anyone, so I don't. "What," she asks, "should I do?"

I want to go back in time and listen to one of my lectures. What could I have possibly said?

Daddy will not allow me to me go to her house. He tells me he doesn't like her stepfather, doesn't trust him. He says, "He is a bad man." I say, "But he hates Black people, and I'm not Black, so it will be okay." I'm desperate to see my friend, who has moved far enough away I can't see her unless Daddy drives me there. Daddy tells me he's sorry but I'm not going. "A racist," he says, "is a racist."

Back then I don't know what he means. Now I do.

Soon after that, we get the late-night call. It is my friend, and she is at the hospital. Her bad stepdad shot her mother in the head and left her for dead. Then he turned the gun on himself. He died. The mother recovers. Looking back, the signs were there. I can still hear my friend's shaky voice on the phone.

This story began because of the night in the beige apartment. But the stories tangle together, folded into my brain like small squares of letters. They run together like ink on the page.

After the night in the beige apartment, you stop eating, stop going to school. You teach me how to erase the skin on the back of my hand with a pencil eraser. Then I see the horror in my parents' eyes. *What?* I think. I don't understand their horror. What's the big deal? I can erase myself! But they make me promise I'll never do it again, and I don't. The scar stays for a long time.

If I look hard enough, I can still see a trace of the scar now.

You dig words into your skin with a razor. And you keep trying to erase yourself, bleach yourself out. The bleach burns your esophagus. You go to the hospital. Daddy takes me to see you, and we make jokes, never talking about why you are there. But I try to imagine it: you holding your nose, putting the white plastic jug to your lips. Drinking the bleach.

One of the letters asks me if I had to succumb to "Well?" again with this new boy. It's a code, of course, but even all these years later, I know what it means without having to think about it.

I am at his house, my neighbor's. There are three brothers, and the middle one circles me once I hit puberty—I can see that now. Other neighbors have hired this boy to water their plants while they are gone. I go with him into these strange houses, bring in the mail, water the plants, and then we make out on waterbeds and couches. One afternoon we are sitting on an overstuffed couch, and something like *Gilligan's Island* or *The Twilight Zone* is on TV. We are watching a little and kissing a lot, and then he pulls down his pants—it's the first erect penis I have ever seen. And he says, "Well?" I am not sure what he means, so he leans back and tells me to suck it. I am thirteen, and I still do not know this is something people actually do to each other, though by now I have heard of it. He must have given me further instruction. But I am gagging, so I stop and say, "Okay. That's enough." I smooth my hair, and he sits there for a while with his pants down. He continues the neighborhood housesitting business without me. I'm unsure what I did wrong. I don't know about ejaculation, not until later.

After the beige night, another friend wonders why you won't come to school. Then she writes, "She's acting weird. Maybe she doesn't like me?" I do not know what I write back. I do know you have too many truancies, so you are not allowed to come back to school. We lose track of you. I lose you. We graduate without you. I learn later your first baby comes at eighteen.

I try to find you over the years in that half-assed way people do when they really aren't sure they want to find what they're looking for. Until the story of the Supreme Court judge enters the news cycle. Then I am desperate to find you. To find out what has become of you. It feels like an excavation.

I google you until I find the obituary. But I tell myself it isn't you even though it is your name and the right age. I find your sister on Facebook, and I wonder if she remembers me, ask her to put me in touch with you. She writes back to me, saying, "Of course I remember you." Then she apologizes for having to tell me they lost you in 2012. You were forty-one. She says the chemical dependencies were too much. Your body finally gave out. She says you left five beautiful children. I write back and tell her terrible things happened to you when we were girls, how I wished I had said something. Your sister says they learned these things through your various hospitalizations. I wonder what they learned, but I know better than to ask. We are still speaking in code.

I read letter after letter, crying for you. Crying for us both.

I remember one night when I am staying over at your house, and you ask me to come inside your closet. You sometimes read in there. I do not think this is strange because I sometimes read on the bathroom floor when Daddy is yelling. I like the way the door locks and the bathroom fan whirls his loud anger away. You have written all over the closet walls. I am surprised by this because that isn't something my own parents would have allowed—writing on walls. You invite me to write something, and I do. I write that I heart the boy from the beige bathroom. You point to your own words. They say, "_____ fucked me."

_____ is your mother's boyfriend. At first I don't understand, and then I do. I keep that in a container inside a container. Though later I remember trying to tell this secret to Daddy. I can't imagine how I would have put it. Daddy drank, but when he wasn't drinking, he was kind. I want to ask him if I told him. If that memory is right. But I can't even ask my mother now, who might have known. And I can't ask you. Everyone's dead.

In another letter a friend complains about you. She says, "I just wished she liked someone else. Now I don't have a chance. She will do anything with a guy, you know she will." There is no date on the letter. I do not know if this is before or after the beige night.

I write to this friend, ask if she remembers you. *Yes, of course.* Then I ask if she remembers this truth you showed me in the closet. She writes back and says you had a difficult home life, that your house was *not a warm place to be.* She is still using the euphemisms. I wonder who she is protecting. I tell her you died. She writes back and says she will be sad all day. "Me too," I say. Me too.

I don't ask any more questions.

Three years after the beige night, after I have lost track of you, I am on my graduation trip, drinking Blue Hawaiians on a booze cruise. I meet a college boy—he is spending his summer break from Harvard in Hawaii. He's a lacrosse player. His rented room is outside of the tourist district, miles away from my hotel. The room smells like cigarettes, incense, and surfboard wax. He pushes me onto the bed and tries to pull off my dress, and when I tell him no, he says, "What did you think? We were coming here to talk?" I am too embarrassed to say yes, I thought we would talk and maybe kiss.

Before I can explain myself—because it's always the girl's job to explain herself—he pins my arms to the bed, telling me I'm a "cocktease." The only reason I get away is because he is drunker than me, and I manage a lucky strike with my foot to his groin—I am a strong girl who has taken her track workouts seriously.

Or maybe remembering you, wrapped in a beige blanket, terrifies me enough to give me strength.

Does this lacrosse player from Harvard—now a middle-aged man in a suit—remember that night in Hawaii? Maybe he sees it as a small folly of his boyhood. Maybe he was blackout drunk. I don't know. I will never know.

I do not know if the boys remember that night in the beige room, though many years later, during the Supreme Court nomination, I mention these memories on Facebook, and every one of the boys (now men) I remember being there immediately block me. Also, I can still see them in my mind's eye, hurrying from the apartment, leaving you there, wrapped in the beige blanket. I remember you getting dressed and us walking to the train trestles and sitting together on a bridge. I remember thinking that if my parents find out I am out on a train trestle late in the night, they might actually ground me. Or worse. I do not want to be there, but somehow I don't say anything because I know you need me to be there.

Maybe I am still woozy from the wine coolers. Maybe you smoke a cigarette. Maybe the train comes. Maybe the coastal fog creeps in, fetid in its salty decay. I don't remember. I only remember this: we look out over the tracks, our feet dangling, and we say nothing at all.

My Mother's Daughter

The day after Mother dies, her boyfriend sits on her patio and weeps. I give him a beer mug, some BBQ tools, tell him she wanted him to have them—I make that up, but I know she would want me to do this, making her look generous and kind. Then he asks me for the patio furniture set, where they had sat together so often. I imagine his wife sitting on the cushion where Mother once sat. I say, "It's spoken for." Another lie. I tell myself I have to choose the items carefully so his wife won't suspect. But more than anything, even with her dead, I have to remember, I am still my mother's daughter. He turns the mug over and says, "Your mother was always so thoughtful," and I agree. Right outside my peripheral vision, I see my mother there, and she's smiling.

Funerals, Safety Pins, and Flaming Saddles

"Oh no," I said when I saw them through the peephole. "No, no, no."

"What is it, darling?" My friend Sholeh asked, coming to the door. I was having my mother's funeral—a garden party—in her backyard.

"It's my mom's boyfriend," I said, now standing with my back against the door. The doorbell rang again. I could hear my mother's voice in my head, saying, *Look what you've done now. Don't open the door!*

Sholeh said, "Why don't you let him in?"

I whispered to her, "He's here with his wife."

"Honey, you have to open the door."

"I do?"

She nodded. "Yes, you do. You invited him."

I opened the door, putting on the biggest, fakest smile I could, forgetting I didn't have to. I was, after all, a girl who had just lost her mother. Larry introduced me to his wife, we shook hands, and I wondered if she knew. She had to know, right?

If I hugged him, his wife would wonder why we knew each other so well. I could hear my mother's voice: *A woman's got to have her secrets. You had better not tell mine.*

We stood there in the doorway, my mom's jade tree now in Sholeh's entry way, and Sholeh said, "Invite them in, darling."

"Yes, yes. Won't you come in?"

"Sorry we're so early. We didn't know how long it would take to drive to LA."

Mother lived in Thousand Oaks, and Los Angeles is only about thirty minutes away, but people in the suburbs always imagine the journey is much farther, and in truth, with traffic it can be. But this was a Saturday, and Larry and his wife were a full thirty minutes early to our garden party funeral. My husband had just gotten out of the shower, and he emerged from the guest room. I walked up to him and whispered through a forced smile, "Tom, I need you to take them into the yard and make small talk with them. I can't do this right now."

Larry said he was coming, but we didn't think he would bring his wife. Tom knew Larry from before, said hello, and then realized why I was unhinged. Larry introduced Tom to his wife. "Can I get you a drink?" Tom asked. They walked over to the drink table, and all of a sudden I was sweating. I told Sholeh, "Get me a towel. I need a towel." She ran off to fetch me one. I felt like the inside of my body was on fire. I didn't know what was going on; I thought I was just nervous. I wiped myself off with Sholeh's towel and didn't realize until later that I was having the first hot flash of my life.

It's a cruel joke that menopause kicks in right around the time our parents are dying.

Tom sat in the garden with Larry and his wife, talking about who knows what. Sholeh said, "You have a good husband."

That's when the basket flew off a top shelf in Sholeh's kitchen. It came crashing to the floor, and hundreds of safety pins scattered across the red tiles. Sholeh and I looked at each other, and she said, "That was your mom."

Sholeh and I kneeled together on her kitchen floor to collect the safety pins, and I didn't know what to think: the scattering of sharp things; the way they hold everything together. Wasn't my mother that sharp-tongued, practical woman, the kind of person who would, in fact, have a spare safety pin in her purse in case the need for one ever arose?

But the haunted scattering? Was she here to say I needed to get my act together?

I would later find out Tom talked to Larry and his wife about our recent trip to Hawaii, the trip my mother and I were supposed to take together, though she was too sick, so Tom and I went together a few days after she died. She had insisted we go, so we did.

Later that night I would go to a Wild West–themed gay bar in West Hollywood with Sholeh, my friend Andy, and his boyfriend Rob. Tom, being the sensible one, stayed home and went to bed. Andy was my instigator, my partner in crime, and my mother's date to my wedding; she called him her "dancing partner." She loved him, and he loved her.

I don't know if we ended up at the Flaming Saddles, where the most beautiful people in the world danced on tables and sometimes swung from ropes, because I was trying to connect with my dead mother, a self-proclaimed "good-time girl," or if I just wanted a reason to get drunk, look at beautiful people, and dance. To do something in opposition to my grief.

I'm not sure how I managed it, but at the club I hoisted myself onto their high tables—the only middle-aged lady in sensible sandals and horn-rimmed glasses climbing into the forbidden territory of beautiful men. And even though it was clearly against the rules, these jeans-and-cowboy-hat-clad men, maybe sensing my brokenness, escorted me down to the dance floor in the gentlest of manners, leaving me with a quick peck on the cheek.

And then I cried to a gigantic drag queen named Pickle. I think she said something like this: "Honey, you need to go home and go to bed."

And you know what? She was right.

But before the late-night gay bar, before I could face the garden party my mother wouldn't have wanted, I cried to Sholeh. We were in her guest room, my mom's friends already in Sholeh's garden, including my mother's married boyfriend and his wife, and I said, "My mom didn't want this party. I did this for me, not her. She wouldn't want this, and she would be mad at me." Although my mother loved attention, she always made sure she controlled it, or at least felt like she was in control. And people sitting around talking about her when she wasn't there? Never. She refused to have any kind of funeral or celebration for my father when he died, and I had always felt a lack of closure. I could still hear her voice in my head: *Well, that's your problem then, isn't it?*

I knew from the start that having this party was going against her wishes. I had left my job and my husband to take care of her for the eight months of chemotherapy and radiation, helping her hide the seriousness of her illness from everyone, including Larry, whom at one point she told she had been cured.

But also, my mother always told me this: "Do what's best for you," and now I was. I wanted to have a party. Even if I could still hear her voice in my head, I wanted some recognition she was, in fact, gone. I told myself because of this she would have relented or at least forgiven me.

But one thing is certain: she wouldn't have wanted Larry and his wife there, and to be fair, Larry couldn't have come without his wife. My mother and Larry ran in the same social circles, and there would be too much talk if Larry attended her funeral alone. But he loved my mother, and I had created an uncomfortable situation, or at least that's what I heard mother saying: *Just look at what you've done now.*

"Listen, honey," Sholeh said. "There are two possibilities here. Your mom is either gone and doesn't know anything about this, or she is somewhere else and doesn't give a damn about what we're doing here because she's moved on. That's all. Those are the only two possibilities." I considered what Sholeh said, and though this made sense, I thought of the third possibility: my mother really was responsible for those safety pins scattering on the floor. She was pissed, unchanged by her ethereal state, and she wasn't about to let me forget it.

When a safety pin is open, it is dangerous. When clasped shut, it is safe, and it is useful.

My mother had suffered the way all people with metastatic lung cancer suffer, maybe even more than most because she had terrible health insurance and bad doctors. But she never cried in front of me and certainly not in front of Larry. Being open would have been too difficult. She couldn't let Larry in, at least not in any meaningful way. She couldn't let me in either.

Since she died, I have tried to get to know her, through her letters and her journals, her souvenirs and photographs. I have attempted to re-create my mother as woman. I have written our story, and every time I do, I cry, prompting my mother to say this: *If it makes you cry, write about something else.* But she also says this: *Who wouldn't want to read about me?*

The day after the garden party, I am back in Mother's house, and the roses Larry sent her weeks earlier are dying. The black-fringed petals flutter as I pick up the vase to throw them out.

Those are still good, I hear her saying, so I set the vase back down on the table.

The Good-Time Girl

"You aren't really going to ring that bell, are you?" Tom asks because this isn't the sort of thing he would normally do.

"Free tours," I say and press the doorbell.

"Oh my God," he says. "You really did it."

The door opens with a creak, and before us stands a woman in her midfifties. She's got a mouth full of yellow teeth, and she's shaped like a bulldog. She looks us both up and down, smiles wide, and asks us what she can do to help us.

"We would like a free tour," I tell her. I'm holding my journal and pen, and if she thinks this is strange, she doesn't say so. We have been on a road trip from Las Vegas to Reno, along Highway 95, also known as the Free-Range Art Highway. I'm a travel writer, and my assignment is to write about the art along the way—the neon and murals of Vegas, the Goldwell open-air art museum, the International Car Forest of the Last Church. The Alien Cathouse is not on the list, but as soon as I see the pink-and-green building at the edge of the desert, I shout, "Stop. Stop the car."

The kitschy Area 51 Alien Center offers gasoline, but you can also buy a stuffed green extraterrestrial toy, take a photo with the resident aliens, or set off fireworks. Next door to the gas station and diner is the Alien Cathouse, a brothel advertising free tours, hot girls, and cold beer.

The stout woman rings another buzzer in code—two short beeps followed by a long one, and I wonder if she's signaling there's a middle-aged couple at the door. We wait for whatever is going to happen next. The Cathouse is inside a converted trailer, like most of the brothels in Nevada. There's a small bar in the corner, where two men flip through notebooks holding pictures of women, the "Cosmic Kittens" on offer. Beer bottles sit in front of them. When the woman notices my gaze, she asks, "Want a drink?"

"Oh, no thank you," I say.

From one of the hallways comes a tall, muscular woman with platinum blonde hair, cut into a pageboy but shaved on one side.

The woman who opened the door says, "This is Lily Grace. She will give you a tour."

Lily smiles and puts her hand on her side, where a waist might be. She's thin but built like a mighty tree. Her lingerie, slit up both sides, displays various tattoos—green roses and peacock feathers. She teeters on Cinderella high-heeled glass slippers, but her feet are far from dainty. The red polish on her toenails is chipped.

Her painted lips spread wide, revealing braces with tiny rubber bands. She asks us how we're doing, and we say just fine. I try to hide my little notebook, though I want nothing more than to write down all the details. I will myself to remember them instead.

She asks us where we're coming from, in a deep voice, and Tom tells her Las Vegas, though I think she means where we live, so I say, "We're on our way home from Vegas. We live in Tahoe." Tom shoots me a look, like I shouldn't have revealed where we're from.

"Where are you from?" I ask her. I smile like I have been caught doing something I wasn't supposed to be doing.

"Texas," she says, smiling like she's doing exactly what she's supposed to. She waves us to follow. Her forearms are strong, like a rock climber's.

We come to a room with flowered curtains and a massage table in the middle. "The showers are over there, and we have a spa for foam parties," she points, "and through there is a bungalow, where you can stay for seventy-five dollars a night."

I ask if people ever just come for a massage, and she says, "That would be a pretty expensive massage. It's usually an add-on."

We follow her through the wood-paneled hallway. There's a photograph of a man with a few Cosmic Kittens. I ask who it is. "Oh, that's the old owner," she says. Tom looks at the picture. "Isn't that Dennis Hof?" he asks.

"Yeah," Lily says. "He died last year."

"How do you know who that is?" I ask Tom.

"He ran for office and won the primary but died before the election."

Lily shrugs. "He was on HBO too." Then she looks directly at me and asks, "Do you want to come to my bedroom and see my prices?"

Before Tom can shake his head no, I say, "Yes, let's!"

Lily motions for us to follow her, and we do. We head back down the hall, and she points to two closed doors. "Those are the suites," she says, "but they're occupied." We come to a dark room in the corner of the trailer. It has an attached bathroom and looks like a cheap motel room. The shiny silver bedspread is crumpled on the bed. A fishbowl full of condoms, a bottle of massage oil, and a box of Kleenex sit on the nightstand. Another bottle that reads "Good Head Deep Throat Spray" is on the bathroom counter, and I want to ask what it is, but I don't dare. Stuffed animals sit atop the dresser, and after my assignment is written and turned in, this is the detail I can't stop thinking about. That and my mother.

My mother grew up poor in northern England, so poor they received oranges in their Christmas stockings, not toys or clothes. I tell people her childhood was like *Angela's Ashes*, only British instead of Irish. She grew up in the postwar days in a coastal resort town, where everything was rationed. They had an outhouse and used newspaper for toilet tissue. My mother worked two jobs—the laundry during the day and a chip shop at night—but her parents took her wages. She had nothing of her own, except for her beauty, and maybe even that didn't belong solely to her.

The chip shop owner had a wife called Bobbie, who had a blonde bouffant hairdo and drove a green Jaguar. She took an interest in my young mother, started inviting her out to the pub and introducing her to older men. They bought my mother drinks and dresses, took her out on the town and to country houses in Spain and France. I once asked my mother if they gave her money, and she said they did but then added, "I wasn't a hooker, you know."

"What were you?" I asked.

"I was a good-time girl," she said.

Years later I would read Jeanette Winterson's books. She writes about the prostitutes in her northern British town, very close to where my mother grew up; Winterson calls these prostitutes "good-time girls." When I came across this description, I read the line again and again, knowing it revealed something essential, the key that unlocked my mother's secret history.

I never had the courage to ask my mother directly, but once when I wrote about it in a poem, she made me take out a line about the men giving her money. "But it was true," I said. She agreed that it was but said it didn't belong in a poem. And maybe it didn't, so I cut the line.

Eventually, a much older married man took a liking to my mother and kept her on as his mistress. "What did Bobbie say?" I asked.

"She was pissed," Mother said.

"Why?"

"Because she lost her girl."

This older man became possessive, even if he was married, and he had my mother followed by a private investigator.

By then my mother had saved her money, bought a car, and moved out of her parents' house. She made a plan and flew to Los Angeles. She told this man she would be back, but within a few days of being in California, she met my father. I only heard this story in the last years of her life, and when I finally heard the truth, or at least this version of it, my mother's coquettishness and her shame, her refusal to go back home, the fierce way she held her secrets, and the way my father protected her finally made sense as if the missing pieces of a puzzle fit into place. There will always be other parts missing, but the picture came into view. I've always wished I could go back and meet that young woman, the one who did what she had to do to escape.

I can still hear Mother's voice: *I wasn't a hooker, you know.* But also she had said this, "Why would I give it away for free?"

The Alien Cathouse sits in the Amargosa Valley, minutes from the nuclear test site in Mercury. There are no other houses around, so I ask Lily if she lives there, at the brothel.

"I'm here one month on, one month off," she says, "so this is my bedroom for now."

"And when you're here, you're always at work. You don't get a break?" I picture her sleeping in the bed with the wrinkled bedspread.

"I work while I'm here," Lily says and picks up a laminated sheet of paper from the dresser. She offers it to us. Tom backs away, but I take it and read it with great interest. An hour with Lily is one thousand dollars. A whole night is eight thousand, and there are various add-ons, like oral, massage, showering, and schoolgirl. I glance at the open closet where different costumes hang—an angel, a maid, the schoolgirl. Ropes and handcuffs hang from a nail on the wall. I ask, "Do many people choose the entire night option?"

Lily shakes her head and says, "Most just buy an hour or two, but every once in a while, someone hits a jackpot in Vegas and they just want to have fun."

I want to stay there and ask questions about her life. How did she end up there? What does her family think? How does she feel about her work? I know that further objectifies Lily, and my voyeurism seems like the worst kind of curiosity porn. But she is saved from my interrogation because Tom thanks her and tells her we have to get going. Lily has taken my curiosity for interest, and when she sees that we're leaving, her face falls. She says, "Are you sure you don't want a drink?"

"No thanks. We have to drive. But thank you so much for the tour," I say.

Lily shrugs again and says, "I'm here if you change your mind."

The two men are still browsing the catalog of Cosmic Kittens when we pass them again to leave.

We thank the woman at the door and walk into the hot wind of the Nevada desert. Tumbleweeds roll past us in the parking lot—I know these plants are Russian thistle: transplants here, nonnative species that have come in time to define this landscape, though it's a place they don't belong.

We climb back into the car and head south on 95. I should be taking notes about the route, researching the next stop on my list, but instead, I stare out the window, thinking about the dark wood-paneled room, the crumpled polyester bedspread, the stuffed toy animals, their plump, pastel bodies doubled in the dresser mirror.

Cloud shadows float across the desert, and the occasional dust devil swirls into being for a few seconds and then disappears.

Later I am still thinking of Lily Grace, so I google her. And there she is, quoted in an article about the new sex robots at the Alien Cathouse. While some of the other Cosmic Kittens worry robots will replace them, threaten their job security, Lily is indifferent. She says, "Most customers come in for the human interaction. I often hear the best part is cuddling after sex." Also, she's moved on from the Alien Cathouse and is now a "courtesan" at the world-famous Bunny Ranch.

I want to believe in the grace of those words: courtesan, good-time girl, a sweetheart known for cuddling.

What She Must Do

A woman in a white button-down shirt, jeans rolled up to her knees, throws a manuscript into the sea, page by page. Some of the sheets return with the current, and she shoves the soggy pages back and back. But they keep returning. She sits in the sand with her head on her knees. Conch shells litter the beach, some whole, some rotted, exposing pink and white rib cages. The mushy papers curl around her feet, and she cries. I want to tell her she must eat each white page, one by salty one, let the ink catch in the vault of the throat, fill the stomach's grave, crowd the tomb of her heart.

OTHER DIFFICULTIES

I don't want to die without any scars.

—CHUCK PALAHNIUK

Animal Bodies

Before seeing the caged meat dogs in Vietnam, we were hiking the coast-to-coast trail across England, and in the mornings we went for the English breakfast. When in England, we had said. But I couldn't eat the blood sausage or the uncooked bacon, not because of the animal behind the meat. I just didn't like it. Until finally, we stayed at a farm, and the bacon was more like we were used to in America, fried to a brown crisp. I told my husband it was the best bacon I had ever eaten, and it was.

Before setting off on our hike that day, I visited the animals around the farm. The cows greeted me at the gate, shoving their noses through the metal bars and licking my hands with their rough tongues. I headed over to the pigs, opened the creaky top of the barn door. The light fell onto the pink bodies, and the pigs scattered and squealed. I watched as they turned to the light, to me, sniffing with their button noses. They approached me with caution. They wiggled their soft ears, blinked into the light with human-shaped eyes.

We hiked across the wet, green grass, and I told Tom I was done eating cows and pigs.

I do not remember how long that lasted, but not long.

When I was a little girl, my mother wanted to get me into kindergarten early, at age four. I had a special interview, testing me to see if I was ready. A nice lady with big glasses administered the test, and I only missed two questions. The first one was whether or not I could cross the street alone. My mother answered that one for me—no, I could not. One has to wonder whether four is old enough for a child to brave the streets of Los Angeles, though this was in 1975, and I had never ridden in a car seat, nor even heard of a seat belt. This was when children routinely rode in the hatchback, or what we kids referred to as "the way back."

The second kindergarten-entry question should have been easy enough: "Where does meat come from?"

Easy! I knew the answer to that. "The grocery store!"

Then I was asked, "Where does meat come from *before* the grocery store?" The lady peered at me through her giant glasses, magnifying her eyes, making her look like an owl. She had a satisfied smile, knowing she had gotten me.

"We buy our meat at the Ralph's," I said.

My mother stuck up for me, saying she didn't think it was a fair question, that Ralph's was, in fact, the correct answer.

"Meat," the examiner explained, "comes from animals. We are eating their muscles." She tugged on her bicep to make sure I understood.

I started to cry, which showed the examiner I understood. I was already an animal lover. I kept rats, parakeets, goldfish, a guinea pig, and a cat as pets. I spent hours watching those industrious little workers in the ant farm my parents bought me. I brought home butterflies with broken wings, hoping to nurse them back to health. I begged for my parents to stop the car when we passed a field of horses or cows so I could get a closer look. I did not want to eat my friends.

I was allowed to start kindergarten in the fall but went on a meat strike.

After becoming a four-year-old vegetarian, I refused to eat meat for many years, though my parents snuck it into dishes, hiding it in spaghetti sauce or casseroles, without my knowledge. I was an indignant child and then an insufferable teenager.

Later I rationalized eating fish, assuming I could kill one with my own hands, though I never had. "If I can't kill it, I shouldn't be able to eat it," I would say. The truth was, I couldn't kill a fish either, so my argument didn't hold water.

Sometime in early adulthood, I started eating meat again. In my memory I was on a road trip with a girlfriend in Telluride, and we were at a BBQ. I smelled the meat, I wanted it, I ate it, and that was that. When I was in my twenties, I could not see my way through to the contradictions—I love animals. I eat animals. Now I understand the many ways I'm a hypocrite, and this is just another example.

Or maybe that's not quite right—the word *hypocrite* comes from the Greek *hypokrites*, meaning "actor" or "to play a part," as in someone who acts in contradiction to stated beliefs. It isn't merely that I am stating beliefs here: I really don't think we should eat animals. So maybe it's more of a paradox—meaning inconsistent with itself yet not obviously untrue. Or maybe like Walt Whitman says, we really do contain multitudes, with the ability to believe two contradictory things at once.

When I met Tom, he did not eat meat. On a trip to see his parents, bratwurst was cooking on the grill. Much like my experience in Telluride, he decided he wanted it, and he ate it, though his ties to meat as a boy growing up in the Midwest were tied to his memories of boyhood. But when we came home, he swore me to secrecy. "Don't tell anyone I ate meat," he said.

"Why do you care?" I asked. "What you eat is nobody else's business."

"Just don't say anything."

I thought it was silly, that if he couldn't let go of his identity as a vegetarian—because it becomes an identity—he shouldn't eat meat. But again, who am I to decide what someone else eats? And maybe his refusal to tell people—perhaps his shame— made more sense than my own about-face years earlier. He understood the moral implications of eating meat, whereas I chose to ignore it.

He now says he didn't want anyone to know because he thought he might go back to being a vegetarian. When I push him, asking "But why?" he says, "It might have been a one-time thing. I just didn't want anyone to know. Stop asking me."

So I stop asking.

At the sprawling Sa Pa market, I look straight on at the cocks fighting, the swayed-back horses meant for meat, the wire cage holding dogs—German shepherds, Siberian huskies, mixed-breed Labs, a white chow chow that looks like my dog, Ely. It is a small enough cage to tie to the back of a motorbike. I cannot count how many dogs are in the small cage because they are a tangled mess of fur, ears, and tails. At least five. Maybe more. The dogs push paws and noses out of the mesh; they pant in the heat, trying not to hurt each other when they adjust themselves but do anyway and yelp out with sharp cries of pain until someone comes and shakes the wire cage. I ask our guide Khu if I can buy them for her. "As pets," I say.

"We have dogs enough," she tells me.

Someone holds a puppy on a leash. "Those are for pets," she says. A man bends down, smacks the small puppy to see if she will submit to him. "Can I buy you one of those?" I ask.

"No," Khu says. "Come on. Let's go."

Khu is Hmong and says they don't eat dogs. "Unless they are very bad," she laughs. I turn to my husband and tell him Ely, a rescue who was known to bite other dogs and sometimes humans, would have been a goner had he lived in Vietnam.

A colleague once told me traveling to India was so sad because of the street dogs. But once I arrived and saw the children begging on the streets, I no longer noticed the dogs.

Until we ran over one.

Sholeh and I were traveling in India, we had hired a driver, and we were pulling up to Mulagandha Kuti shrine. The dog had been sleeping on the street. The dog's cry was sharp and shrill like broken glass. "Oh my God, oh my God," I said. The driver stopped, and I jumped out of the car. The dog managed to get up and stood on three legs, howling. The dog's high-pitched cries summoned a pack of street dogs, eight to be exact, to the scene of the crime. I stood against the car, and the dogs circled me, barking in lamentation for their friend's useless leg. The injured dog tried to touch the paw of the smashed leg on the pavement, recoiled in pain. The driver got out and tried to shoo the dogs away, but they wouldn't budge. They stood their ground, circling the car, barking at us. The driver went to charge them, and finally they dispersed. The wounded dog hopped away on three legs.

When we reached the temple, I was already in tears. I knew it had been my fault because if I hadn't been interrogating our driver about his personal life, his eyes would have been on the road. We hadn't thought our driver spoke much English until he asked, "Are you married?"

"I'm not, but she is." I had pointed to Sholeh.

"Were you arranged?" I asked the driver, figuring if he could ask me if I was married, I was entitled to the details of his marriage.

"Yes, I am."

"Please stop talking to the drivers when they're trying to drive," Sholeh had told me. "You're distracting him."

"Yes, we were arranged," he said.

"Do you love her?" I asked, leaning forward.

Sholeh had covered her nose and mouth with her shawl, trying to protect herself from the traffic fumes, but she pulled it down to say, "Suzanne! That's enough."

"She's a good wife. She speaks softly to my parents. Very modest," the driver said, looking into the rearview mirror at me.

That's when we rolled over the dog's leg.

Street dogs were just another part of the fabric of India, along with the blind musicians and the snake charmers, the children begging for one rupee, the feral monkeys, and the cow struggling down the street with a broken leg, which is a sadder sight than a three-legged dog.

Inside the temple—dark and cool and private—I let myself cry briefly before pulling myself together. I wiped my tears away, knowing the driver wouldn't appreciate my crying over a dog. Sholeh was kind enough not to tell me it had been my fault even though I knew it was. At home I would have gone to bed for two days and cried had I been responsible for injuring a dog, but there in India, that felt self-indulgent, and in the end it would do nothing for the injured animal.

I'm sure I'm not the first tourist who visited Vietnam and wanted to save the dogs. Even still, I ask Khu again, "Just one dog?" but she's already passing the water buffalo on her way back to the vegetable market, and we have to jog to catch her. I know that even if I bought the whole wire cage full of dogs intended for meat and set them free, they would be rounded up again for the Sa Pa market next Sunday. I tell myself that we eat pigs and they are cute too and smarter even than dogs.

I once had a student who trained dogs at the local Petco in town. He told me he once trained a pig. "That pig learned tricks faster than any dog I have trained," he said. I asked him if he still ate bacon. "Hell yes," he said. "Why wouldn't I?"

Later I'll be wandering around Virginia City, Nevada, and I will spot a man walking a pig on a leash. I'll jog across the road, chasing after them. "I love your pig," I will blurt out when I catch them.

"I do too," the man will laugh. He is wearing a kilt, Dr. Martens red-and-black combat boots, and a wide silver ring through his septum. "Meet Pepper Murphy," he will say. I'll run my hand along the bristlelike hairs. Pepper will wriggle his ears and seem to be smiling. The man will give me a slice of dried apple, showing me how to hold it out to his pig. Pepper will sit for the treat, and I'll hand it to him. His bottom teeth are sharp fangs, but he will take the fruit gently.

"Such a smart boy," I will say.

"Totally potty-trained and knows tons of tricks. Smarter than my dogs," the man says.

"So I've heard." The man and his pig will be about to walk away, and I'll say, "Can I ask you something?"

"Sure."

"Do you eat pork?"

The man will smile, shake his head, and say, "No. No way. Once you see how these animals are, and even the bigger pigs are the same, you can't eat them."

Even so, why should beauty or intelligence be the measure of an animal's worth? Why is it that we evaluate a life based on these criteria?

Still, I do not want to eat dogs. Or horses or cats or even guinea pigs. I will remember the pigs and the cows at that farm in England. And then wonder at how my moral compass was so much clearer when I was a child, when the world easily divided into right and wrong. But I do not want to think like a child, ignoring the ambiguities of this life, the way I can love animals and still eat them. Pigs and cows have been domesticated for more than ten thousand years. And over those years I join those who have struggled with the ways my own animal nature means I am a mammal who eats other mammals.

And of course, the real problem is not eating animals but the way we treat them before killing them. The disgusting and torturous conditions of factory farming. But that is a separate issue. Or is it?

My friend Tracy lives on a small farm, where she and her children kill ducks and geese, rabbits and goats. She and her husband hunt deer. I know I should ask her if I can come to the farm, watch as she breaks the necks of rabbits. I know that if I am willing to eat meat, I should be able to watch as they are killed, even if I could never kill them myself.

But I can't. Or maybe I can, but would it change the way I eat? I'm not sure. But I do know those images will be in my mind, like the dogs in cages—with me forever, or at least until my own death, my own personal forever. For now I want to save myself from this.

My mother's mother drowned kittens in a bucket in the kitchen. She made my mother—a little girl—help her. Mother told me she still remembered her favorite, a black-and-white one she had named Windy and the way Windy struggled for air, the way her pink nose pushed for the surface of the water, the way my grandmother shoved her small face under until the kitten went limp. Even though I wasn't there, I imagine the fine kitten whiskers, the nose searching for air, then going still. My grandmother also killed Henrietta, the chicken, and Peter, the rabbit—animals my mother believed were her pets.

Mother never stopped eating meat, but her memories, her own love of animals, sat separate from what she ate, like boxes on a shelf. But I suppose we all do this, compartmentalize the difficult things, in some way or another.

When she was dying, my mother wanted a pet. She scanned Petfinder.com, scrolled down until she came to a pig.

"How about a pig?" she asked. "He's looking for his forever home."

My mother was given three months to live. I didn't want to inherit a pet pig. Or rather, I did want to inherit a pet pig, but my husband wouldn't have let me keep it. But still, I played along. "What would you name it?" I asked.

"Porky," she said.

"Maybe we could find him a girlfriend and name her Petunia." We laughed, both knowing we were not going to adopt a pig. Or two.

And no one loved bacon as much as my mother.

As I walk away from those caged dogs in Vietnam, I force myself to turn back, take one last look, before moving on.

But do we ever really move on?

Because there is this: Mother always hated water. She couldn't stand with her head under the shower's spray, so she washed her hair in the sink, leaning back, so her face stayed dry.

The Queen of the Amazon

A toucan hopped along the railing of our ecolodge. I marveled at its bright plumage. I had only ever seen such a bird on a cereal box. I moved closer, but the bird became scared and tried to fly off but couldn't. I realized its wings had been cut, holding it hostage at the ecolodge. The toucan flapped its shorn wings but plummeted into the murky water below. I ran to get our guide, José. He followed me to the spot the bird sank. He peered into the green water, waved his hand, and told me not to worry about it. "Toucans can swim," he said.

I didn't know if that was true or not, so that night I lay awake under the scratchy green netting and worried I had been responsible for killing the bird.

I had wanted to go to Cartagena for our honeymoon because of Gabriel García Márquez, who had once said he completed his education as a writer in Cartagena. It seemed to me that Márquez was the most romantic writer there ever was—I've always been drawn to unrequited love, and *Love in the Time of Cholera* was one of my favorite novels. I had finally found requited love, later in life, and I believed Colombia, and specifically Cartagena, would make the quintessential honeymoon. Tom and I spent most of our travels together backpacking, sea kayaking, or skiing, so adding a trek through the Amazon while we were in Colombia felt like the perfect way to celebrate our new marriage—it was also the way I got him to agree to Colombia. Tom was always up for an adventure.

The Ecolodge Paradiso in Marasha sat on a small lake in Peru, close to the Colombian and Brazilian borders. I had picked it for the economical price and also because it claimed to be environmentally friendly. I had built a life around travel, but also I had recently finished a doctorate in environmental literature and was keenly aware of the negative impacts of our trips to the world and its creatures, both human and otherwise. And though I was well schooled in some ways—maybe just in the world of books—it soon became clear I hadn't done my research when it came to choosing this particular ecolodge.

Tom and I arrived by boat. The wooden buildings sat on stilts in green water. The common areas were outdoors on large decks, with metal roofs overhead to shield visitors from the rainstorms, which came often and with great force. A few other travelers sat around, eating snacks, reading books, or napping in rope hammocks. We were shown the pit toilets and then our room, a wooden cabin with holes between the slats and a scratchy green mosquito net over the small bed. Our door didn't shut all the way, so a curious tapir, also named José, used his long snout to nose his way into our room at all hours.

Our small plane from Bogotá had landed a few days earlier on the grass strip in Leticia, the southernmost city in Colombia and the capital of Amazonas. The fecundity in the air felt chewy in my mouth. I had visited rainforests before but never before had this feeling—that we had entered into the green heart of the earth. We hitched a ride in the back of a truck to the town square, near the hostel I had booked. The smell of diesel and the green jungle made me feel dizzy. A woman in high heels sped by on a moped. I loved everything about this place.

We were dropped off and walked through the park with our backpacks. The pinkish purple twilight fell, and the trees shook with birdsong—both familiar and otherworldly. I looked up, and hundreds of yellow-and-green parakeets darted from the trees. I had only ever seen parakeets in cages, like the blue and yellow birds I kept as a child—Howard and Tweety Bird. Howard was so stressed out in captivity he plucked his own feathers from his chest. I thought about the way animals so often suffer in our hands. But these birds were wild and free and full of song. The sun sank below the flat horizon, the sky turned gray, and Tom wanted to find our hotel. I stood there for a few more minutes, my eyes closed, listening to the bright-green uproar of the parakeets' song.

"Did you know," I asked Tom, "that a flock of parakeets is called a pandemonium?"

"I didn't," Tom said in the way he answers me when I have asked him a question I already know the answer to.

We bought ice cream cones and ate them as we wandered through the park and toward the small but busy town. Bats swooped overhead, and the evening filled with the buzz of cicadas and then the pouring rain.

We spent the next day walking around Leticia, peering into creature-filled buckets for sale at the markets. A man squeezed hot sauce onto a live grub and ate it. I told myself different is just different—not strange, not gross, but different, so I ordered fried grubs that evening at a restaurant. Maybe they were delicious? I would never know unless I tried them.

The waitress told me they were out of them. But, she added, they did have fresh ones. In my mind it was one thing to eat the grubs cooked and another thing entirely to eat them while they squirmed, so I shook my head, and we ordered a local fish instead. Tom got the tail, and I got the head. I asked the server if we could have the middle, and she said they didn't have any fillets left. Tom laughed and asked, "How would you have been able to eat the worms if you can't even eat a fish head?"

That didn't seem like a question that deserved an answer, so I sat quietly looking at my fish head in the dim light.

"I'll switch with you," he said and traded his plate for mine. "You can't say I never made any sacrifices for you."

"And you can't say I didn't give you head on our honeymoon."

Tom pulled the flesh from the fish's cheek with his fork and said, "You're funny."

"Looks aren't everything," I said and stared down at my tail, seeing it wasn't any better than the head.

After the public boat ferried us from Leticia to the ecolodge, we met José, our personal guide for the week. We dropped our backpacks off in our cabin, and José took us on an evening boat ride to look for caimans and monkeys. Rain clouds piled black and gray against the horizon. Other guided boats full of tourists cruised across the water. We trolled around the small green lake in a misty rain. José shined a flashlight into the trees, and we heard a rustle. He unpeeled a banana, held it into the air like a trophy, and monkeys leaped into the boat. They jumped onto our shoulders and heads, used to this nightly show for tourists and the delicious treats they received for participating. José encouraged us to take pictures of each other with the monkeys.

The sky shifted from gray to black, and José trained his light onto the dark lake and then, with one quick movement, netted a caiman, which looked like a tiny alligator. He wrangled it, holding its snapping mouth shut so we could have a look. He tied twine around its jaws so it couldn't plunge its sharp fangs into him. The yellow teeth clenched in an overbite, and the greenish eyes flashed with what seemed to be anger or fear. The caiman was about two feet long, and I asked if it was a baby.

José said yes, they can grow to five meters. Would I like to hold him? I looked into the black water below and said, "No gracias."

We walked back from the wooden dock, and I told Tom I was afraid the lodge I had chosen wasn't very ecologically friendly, that I didn't like the way they treated the animals. Tom told me the monkeys were fine, that José had thrown the caiman back, unharmed. I hadn't yet told Tom about the toucan with the clipped wings I had scared into the water earlier that day.

"What are you? The Queen of the Amazon?" Tom asked.

José handed us each a pair of rubber boots for our morning trek through the rainforest, where he pointed out leaf-cutter ants and blue morpho butterflies. We walked through fields that had been slashed and burned to grow corn, bananas, and plantains, where the lush smells of green jungle were replaced by a burnt yellow.

Butterflies as big as my hand flitted in the sunlight; egrets followed cows through the pasture. The earth had been reduced to ash beneath our boots. The noontime sun glowed in the sky, the air no longer burdened by the weight of water and vines; instead, it felt hot and dry, a different climate, mere steps away from the wet, dark jungle. The saw-chewed stumps of four-hundred-year-old ceiba trees scattered among the banana trees and plantains. The wood, jagged along their hollow shoulders— they reminded me of dead grandmothers. Ceiba trees were sacred to the Mayans, who believed they were a symbol of the universe: the roots burrowing to the underworld, the trunk representing the human-dwelling middle world, and the branches reaching to the heavens.

My eyes stung and watered. I told myself I couldn't cry over someone else's trees. I didn't stop to ask myself to whom the trees belonged; I didn't have the words for my deep feelings of unease and loss, which I now recognize as ecological or environmental grief, a term that would not be common for another five years—the deep sadness, mixed with the helplessness, we feel when faced with environmental degradation and disaster.

But even still, I tried to put the words of my limited Spanish vocabulary to my feelings, telling our guide José that this plantation, this pasture, was ugly. "And so very sad," I said.

"Es la verdad, pero la gente—ellos no pueden comer los àrboles."

I translated for Tom: "The people—they cannot eat the trees." Then I turned to José and asked, "It's complicated, isn't it?"

José laughed, shook his head, and walked on. I didn't say anything else to the guide, and because Tom couldn't speak Spanish, we walked together in silence, the scorched grass crackling beneath our rubber boots. Each small town was surrounded by slash-and-burn agriculture, and we ended our trek in one such village, the tiny Puerto Alegría in an area called Tres Fronteras, where Peru, Colombia, and Brazil meet on the Amazon River. Water-stained wooden houses sat on stilts, a hint of what it's like in the rainy season, when an average of twelve inches of rain fall per month.

José brought us each a soda with a plastic straw and asked us to sit. That's when the children came. So many children, each holding a baby animal. Turtles, snakes, birds, two sloths. They thrust the animals at us. "For photographs," José said. I took a picture of all the children, and a little girl pushed a baby sloth onto my chest. The small animal gripped my shirt. I could feel its heart racing. Even though sloths don't move fast—hence their name—and their markings make them look perpetually happy, I knew this animal was terrified.

I tried to give the sloth back to the child, but it clung to me with its three clawed toes. The little girl waited for her *propinita*. I knew giving her money would perpetuate this, but how could I refuse? I was holding her sloth, so I owed her a little tip. I was a bad tourist either way.

I couldn't reach for the change in my pocket because of the sloth I was holding, so I said, "Tom, please give her some money." He handed over a tip, and I pulled the claws of the sloth from my shirt and handed the animal back. I told José in Spanish I didn't want to hold the animals.

"Don't be afraid," he said and laughed.

"It isn't that," I said. "I'm not scared. I'm sad."

By now more guides had brought more tourists here to join us. Another woman took the small sloth from the girl and asked her boyfriend to take pictures. Another man held an anaconda. The other tourists seemed unbothered by this cruel show, delighted even, but perhaps I seemed that way from the outside too.

A sloth should sleep twenty hours a day, so these tourist visitations are so stressful for them that they often die within six months of being captured. The snakes go blind from the constant camera flashes. Even though I didn't know these gruesome details at the time, I was unhappy about the situation, but I didn't know how to get out of it once I was there.

While the other tourists snapped photos with the animals, I sat away from them on a tree stump. A woman walked toward me with a spotted cat on a leash. She called it a baby jaguar, but it was a margay, a smaller cousin to the ocelot. Before I could stop her, the woman plopped the wild cat in my lap. It was about twice as large as a house cat, with shiny, spotted fur. I pet the animal, not knowing how to respond to its wildness, knowing only how to respond to a domesticated cat. The animal purred. The guide walked over to me and said, "See, she's happy. And the sloths, couldn't you see they were smiling?"

José told Tom to take my photo, and he did, making the Queen of the Amazon joke again. In the photograph I smiled weakly, an accomplice to this crime. I motioned for the woman to take the cat. My lap was still warm, and she waited for her tip. I reached into my pocket and handed her some change.

There were no border controls on the river in Puerto Alegría, which had facilitated wildlife trafficking and made it difficult for authorities from three separate countries to address the situation. I could say it was complicated again, walk on, and eventually go home, but didn't the jungle belong to José and the woman with the baby margay? To the children? No matter how much we travel, we can never understand other places like we know our own home. But isn't it also true that the jungle belongs to both everyone and no one?

By the time we returned to the lodge, we were hot, insect pocked, and our damp clothes smelled like mildew. An angry rash crawled up my legs from hiking all day in the rubber boots. I took a cold shower and then sat on the deck, overlooking the lake, and wrote in my journal.

Red parrots with shorn wings scrabbled across the deck railings nearby. After what had happened with the toucan, I kept my distance. I wrote that we should have stayed in Bogotá, the beautiful mountainside city with the museum of voluptuous Boteros. Or headed to Cartagena earlier, with its marble-floored cathedral, umbrella-shaded outdoor tables, and lively street performers. I wrote: *The honeymoon is over.* I didn't mean my honeymoon with Tom was over; I meant something deeper than that. I had heard about the destruction of the Amazon, but when you are far away from something, you can't really picture what that means. It's like hearing about a death toll in the thousands. It's impossible to parse out each individual life in such a large number. But here I could see each life. The tropical birds with shorn wings; the leashed wild cat; a captured baby owl, skittery and confused, the yellow eyes like marbles. I wrote into my journal: *How long can a nocturnal creature stay awake before it dies? Is it true that toucans really can swim?*

Just then, I looked up, and a group of tourists gathered around a baby manatee, caged in the water near the ecolodge. José took the animal out of the water, and the tourists took turns holding her. Another baby stolen, another animal mother in grief.

I went back to my journal but started writing about our recent wedding. When I look back at these pages, it seems like a strange shift, but it had been too much—I had always wanted to see a manatee but not like that.

José took us on another boat tour, this time to visit another small village, where the residents were running yucca through a grinder. A woman led us into a raised wooden cabin with colorful hammocks crisscrossing the room. On the ground a caiman on a leash scrabbled across the plywood floor. I wondered how long it could live out of the water. She also had a nocturnal monkey, which she released onto my head. I screamed, and she laughed. The animal clung to my hair, and she asked for the equivalent of seventy-five cents, which we handed over.

It would take me a decade to return to these memories, three years after *National Geographic* ran an article, leading to the confiscation of twenty-eight wild animals in the village we had visited. But how long would it be before the villagers replaced them? Tourist tips are lucrative, especially in an economy where the average salary was less than U.S. $250 per month.

The people—they cannot eat the trees.

I look at the photographs of me holding the margay, of the monkeys on my head, and I am deeply ashamed—it doesn't matter that it made me uncomfortable at the time: I held the wild animals and then produced a tip, like all the other tourists did. My new husband dutifully took the photographs when prompted by the guide. There I am, *the Queen of the Amazon*, topped with a monkey crown.

We walked back to the boat, and I told José, "No more animals."

He looked skeptical.

We motored along the river, and José and Tom fished for piranhas. They caught one, and José held it. "Delicious," he said as the fish squirmed. Tom, who enjoys fishing, was unbothered.

"Keep it for your family," I said. "But please kill it quickly." He whacked it on the head with a paddle, but still it flopped around in the bottom of the boat, its fins sucking at the terrible air. Watching it, my heart felt like it flopped around, too, and I repeated, "No more animals."

He took another whack at the fish's head, this time with his machete, and he looked at me. He told me he didn't understand. Hadn't I come to the Amazon, like all the other tourists, to see the diversity of their wildlife?

"No more monkeys or jaguars or sloths or caiman," I said as a way of explanation.

"You don't like them?" he asked.

"Only in the wild," I said. "Not in cages and on leashes."

"You will only see them that way," he said. "You would not see any of these animals in the wild." The fish stopped flopping.

"I don't want to see them then. I would rather know they are free out there," I pointed to the jungle on the other side of the river, "than to see them on leashes and in cages."

José shook his head, perhaps worried about his tip. Then he pointed downriver and shouted, "Delfín rosado." A pod of small, bright pink dolphins jumped from the water, making rainbows of the spray. My own heart now leaped with them, and I caught my breath. I had never seen something so unusual, so beautiful, as those pink dolphins. They were the color of bubble gum, bursting from the green river. I stood up in the small boat to get a better look, and José asked me if I liked the dolphins.

"Very much," I said. "I love them." The direct translation from the Spanish would have been "They enchant me very much," which felt more accurate.

"Sit, sit," he said, turning the boat. "We can go closer so you can get a picture."

"No. I have them here." I pointed to my head. "I have them in a picture in my mind."

Tom asked what we were saying, and I told him. Tom nodded and smiled, showing José he didn't need a picture either.

José shook his head again, and I wondered if he was doing the math, the tip he might not receive if I didn't take a photograph of the magnificent pink river dolphins. I said, "I like them best from far away."

"I can't take it anymore," I told Tom, and we left the ecolodge early, even though they wouldn't refund our money.

"Whatever the Queen of the Amazon wants," Tom said.

I found a small hostel in our guidebook called Hotel Napü, farther upriver in Puerto Nariño, and we took a public boat there. We arrived in a downpour, sharing an umbrella that wasn't doing anything to keep us dry in the slanted rain. We walked past colorful houses, along the narrow sidewalks—no motorized vehicles were permitted in the town. The pedestrian-only community was an ecological experiment that had worked, unlike the Ecolodge Paradiso. Men played soccer on the muddy field. A woman stood under a balcony, shouting, "Piñas, bananas, mangos," and we stopped to buy some fruit.

Two little girls, about the same age as those in Puerto Alegría holding turtles and snakes and sloths, splashed into puddles, unbothered by the rain. I watched them laugh with each other in that uncomplicated way only children laugh. They skipped by holding hands, ignoring us. I dropped the umbrella, stood in the pouring rain, and smiled without meaning to, for there was that lightness—the unburdening of terrible things, children playing in the rain, a pandemonium of parakeets lifting into flight.

A True Story about Jealousy

I brought home one of those betta fish, a bluish purple one with long wings who always sits by herself, looking forlorn, in a little round jar at the pet store. Though I had been warned, I put my little purple fish into a big, beautiful tank with lots of other dreamy fish, figuring she was so small, how could she hurt anyone else? At first she ate the tiniest fish and then moved on to the medium-sized fish and then to the frogs (she devoured their little frog arms and legs first) and then the eels and shelled creatures. She grew larger with each body she consumed, finally swallowing the biggest fish in the tank. I watched in horror. She jumped out of the water, which was now too small to contain her, and came after me. She was halfway up my arm, and I was trying, unsuccessfully, to beat her off with a stick when I finally woke up.

The Last Goodbye

The way we loved her—my ex-husband, Craig, and I—ended in a fierce custody battle when we divorced, both of us threatening the other with lawyers and lawsuits. Which, of course, was ridiculous, since animals, as we found out, are not family but property. This meant Riva Jones was technically mine, since I'd adopted her before the marriage. But as we all know, in matters of the heart, *technically* and *legally* are muddled.

When we fought, Riva would come over and rest her head on my knee while she looked up at me, her eyes saying, *Please be happy*. She, like most dogs, was family, not property. And that's why I agreed to share custody of her. My ex loved her the way I loved her, and no matter what kind of meanness I could muster for him at the loss of our relationship, I could not take Riva away from him, nor could I take him away from Riva.

After we broke up, we traded weeks. He lived across the highway, and it was easy enough. We saw her through two major surgeries, costing us seven thousand dollars; she saw us through new partners, engagements, broken engagements, and a marriage. She loved us just the same. She accepted her two-household life. She loved the girlfriends of my ex (even though I told her not to), and she loved my new husband, Tom.

After three years of the weekly dog swap, Craig announced he was moving three hours away. I figured I'd keep Riva full-time, but he figured otherwise and fought for her. Motivated by the leftover guilt of leaving him or the fact that she loved him too, I agreed—we would do the dog swap once a month. For three more years we met on the side of highways, at rest stops, in the dark corners of gas stations. It seemed like we were trading contraband—who would have guessed we had pulled over to trade off a German shepherd?

Tom was annoyed by waiting in gas station parking lots or on the side of the road. I do not know what the girlfriend thought. But Riva always seemed happy to get into one car or the other, never complaining, never even looking back. I wish I had a little bit of that kind of acceptance, that way of living in the moment, the attitude that says: "Okay, this is what we're doing now. Fun!"

At twelve Riva started cutting trail on backcountry ski trips so she could keep up. The last time I took her skiing, she ran down the skin track instead of following behind us, diving in and out of the fresh snow. When she disappeared, I shouted for her for an hour, afraid she'd fallen in a tree well. She had taken the easy way down and was waiting for us at the car; she sat, smiling, as if to say, *That sure took you a long time.*

I took Riva on her last summer hike when she was fourteen, which, in retrospect, was ambitious, though even our vet had called her the "Wonderdog." My plan was to hike the two miles to Meiss Meadow from Carson Pass and then back again. It was hot, she was tired, and her back end kept giving out. I sat in the shade with her, stroked her head, and told her it was okay. I am sure my ex and Riva took a similar hike—one that was a little too much.

By fifteen Riva was blind and deaf. She became incontinent and backed away when she realized what she had done. I tried my best to tell her it was all right. Nobody was mad at her. No one had ever been mad at her. We tried everything, including installing a doggy door and layering plastic over the floor of one room, with pieces of old carpet on top so she wouldn't slip. That lasted until she pooped, stepped in it, and smeared it all over the carpet pieces and the plastic. Then the dog whose bed had been right next to mine for fifteen years had to sleep in the garage.

Craig got a new job, one that required travel, so the last six months of her life, Riva stayed exclusively with me. I resented Craig on the days I had to clean the messes in the house, on my shoes, and in her fur. I resented it every night when I brought her down to sleep in the garage, tucking a blanket around her as she looked up at me with her now cloudy eyes. I resented it every time I had to help her up and down the stairs, every time I had to go outside and stop her from barking at imaginary things, which prompted the neighbors to call animal control, even the police. Once during that time I needed a break and called Craig; he said he couldn't take her. I didn't resent Riva; I resented Craig.

Tom said, "Riva is here to teach you something. It's her last gift."

I made a list of all the things I loved and how many of them I could do without and still want to live. Perhaps I could go without skiing and hiking and running but not reading, not spending time with family and friends. I came up with a number: 30 percent. If I could still do 30 percent of the things I loved, I would want to live.

I made a list for Riva. She could no longer chase chipmunks or swim, but she could eat treats and relax in the sun. From what I could tell, she was at exactly 30 percent. That's when I started googling "When to put your dog down." During this period Brenda came over. When she saw Riva, she said, "You have to put that dog down." She was not being mean; it's just that Brenda was not one to couch her opinions in euphemism. She had an aging pit bull, Daisy, who went everywhere with her; they even went out together last Halloween, both dressed as witches. Brenda said, "When it's Daisy's time, I want you to tell me."

I should also say that in addition to old age, Riva had Cushing's disease, and her spine was a column of stones. Her belly was bloated and her fur matted with old age. Her milky eyes probably no longer looked intelligent, but I had not noticed. At one point that evening, Riva had fallen on the slate floor (recently installed because of her incontinence) and cried, and I picked her up. This from the dog who never complained.

Brenda repeated: "Put that dog down. You can't let a dog lose her dignity." I knew Brenda was right, that she was only trying to encourage me to do the humane thing, but of course, I could think only that *this was coming from a woman who dressed her pit bull in a witch costume.*

I asked Tom what he thought, and he said, "It's your decision to make. And you have to do it alone. Riva would want that from you. She expects it."

I called Craig, and we decided together we would put Riva down in one week's time. Craig would come to my house. The vet would put her down at home. I put in for a day off work. But still, I kept searching online for something that would make things easier, something that would tell me when it was time. Again, I googled "When to put your dog down" and landed upon lists and surveys, which I took for Riva, checking whether or not she ate or wagged her tail when I got home (the answer to both of those was yes, until the very end).

All week I fed Riva steak and chicken and rice. I doubled her pain medication. I spent as much time with her as I could, and she improved. The weather had warmed, so she was sleeping on the deck, happy in the spring sierra air. Some days she could walk a half-mile up the trail behind my house. Craig came over, and we ended up sitting on the deck, sharing a bottle of chardonnay with Riva at our feet. We caught up on our friends but talked very little about Riva. I wondered why he didn't spend the time on the ground with her but figured we all deal with these things in our own way; maybe he didn't really want to admit she was going, could not bear to say goodbye.

Craig came again the next day, the day before the appointment, and we took her for a walk. She made it about a half-mile before needing to turn back. We saw a bear, and she seemed happy to be among the wakening wildlife. We didn't talk about the appointment, which was how things had always been between us. But after he left, I canceled it. I told him we'd wait and see, take it day by day. Craig went home.

In the end it really would be my decision to make. Among the survey questions on the "Should you put your dog down?" test was *Did you make euthanasia appointments and cancel them?* I now checked yes. Riva was now at fifty-fifty, the point at which, according to the survey, one should consider "putting the dog down." But did it count? Did I make a mistake when I made the appointment in the first place? So I waited.

I am here to tell you there will be an answer to your question "When should I put my dog down?" but the answer cannot be found on an internet survey.

There is only this: on a Thursday morning in April, you will wake up, and your dog will be throwing up. By the time you leave for work, she will seem fine. But still, you ask your dog sitter, who is also a vet tech, to check on her during the day. You will run a poetry slam in the evening and will not be home until late. When you call your husband after work and before the event, he will say your dog seems fine. You will ask him what the dog sitter's note said—she always leaves detailed descriptions of what goes on.

"No note," he will say.

"She always leaves a note. Find it. Tell me what it says."

"I didn't see a note."

"Look on the counter," you will insist.

"No note," he will answer.

You will leave it alone, knowing something is wrong, but you are in charge of an event at work, so you choose to believe your husband is telling you the truth.

He isn't. He knows you have to go to the event. The note says your dog has been throwing up. But Tom will have checked on her, and she seems to have improved, so he doesn't say anything.

When you get home, you find your dog on the porch, dry heaving. Though it will not have snowed for a month, on this night it will be snowing. You will find your dog outside, trying to throw up over the deck. She will know better, even then, to make a mess outside. She will be shivering, and tiny frozen flakes will be caught in her fur.

You will coax her inside, start the fire, and ask her to lie on her bed. She will be dry heaving, and every once in a while, yellow bile will come up. She will froth at the mouth, and you will wipe the fur around her face with a towel.

Here is when you know: when it's already too late. Which is what you tried to avoid with your googling late into the night. You will apologize to her over and over, telling her how sorry you are for not having the doctor come to the house and put her down.

But you could not have done that. You needed it to get to this.

You will call your vet, and because you live in a small mountain town, the office is closed. You will be directed to the emergency vet hospital in Reno, more than an hour from your house. You call the hospital, and the woman on the other end of the line will encourage you to bring your dog in. "Her stomach could be flipped, and this is extremely painful," the voice will say. You don't believe this, but it will make you cry harder. "But she probably won't make the drive," the vet tech says.

You will ask, "Why would I force my dog into a long car ride she probably won't make?"

"You should bring her in," the voice on the other end will answer. You will hand the phone to your husband, and he will talk to the vet tech in the other room. You cannot, in fact, do this alone.

When he hangs up and comes back into the living room, you ask if you are going to drive your dog to the big-city vet. He will say no. You will say, "Call Brenda. Ask for her gun."

He will say, "What? I am not calling Brenda. It's after midnight."

"Call Brenda and ask for her gun."

"I can't do that."

"You have to. Just get her gun."

This is when you know it is time to put your dog down: when you have never shot a gun in your life, and you're willing to illegally fire a bullet from your friend's pink .22 into your dog's brain.

Tom will call Brenda, and after she figures out who's calling her so late at night and asking for her gun, she says no way. She tells you it is illegal to shoot a handgun in your town. Level-headed as she is, Brenda will not let you shoot your own dog.

So you pull your dog's bed, with her on it, over to the couch and sleep next to her. She will dry heave for a while but then fall asleep, mercifully, until 7:00 a.m. For the last time you sleep beside her.

Your husband leaves for a meeting. It will seem, for a minute, that your dog has stopped dry heaving, frothing at the mouth.

But she hasn't.

You will call your local vet, and the receptionist says the vet cannot come to the house, but you can bring your dog to the office anytime. Your eyes have that sandpapery feel. You won't know why, but you feel the need to shower while your poor dog is suffering in the other room. Maybe you just want to make sure. Maybe you will get out of the shower and she will have stopped dry heaving and she will be better.

She isn't.

So you dry off and get dressed and realize you can't wait for your husband to be done with his meeting. It is time.

You lift your old dog from her bed and carry her down the stairs. She does not resist you. You put her on the grass, and she sniffs around and goes to the bathroom, and this last act of normal doggy behavior nearly brings you to your knees.

You call her, your voice cracking. She sees the hand motions you now use since she can no longer hear you, and she looks into the car as if she might try to jump into it. Before she can try, you lift her into the car. She smiles, knowing she is going somewhere.

You call your ex, telling him you are on your way to the vet . . . that it is time. You call your friend Eve, who has three dogs, because you figure she might offer you some words of wisdom, and she does. She tells you to have them do it in the car. This is how she has had all her dogs put down.

When you walk into your vet's front office, everyone knows why you're there. The front office staff tells you they will help you carry her in. You look around at all the other pet owners with their animals who will have to watch this. Your vet agrees to come out to the car. You are thankful for your friend who told you to have it done in this way. You go out to the car, open the back, and sit with your dog in the morning sun.

The front-office person comes out with paperwork. He asks if you want your dog's paw print. You imagine them sticking the dead paw into a mold and quickly say no. Then you realize your ex might want said paw print, so you call him.

"Hey, Craig, do you want her paw print?" you say when he picks up.

"Her what?"

"You know, they make a plaster imprint of her paw." Then you add, "But they do it after she's dead."

Your ex will agree that the $79.95 paw print isn't needed and says, "Do the private cremation, okay? And call me. Later."

You agree you will. You know "later" means after.

You also agree to the more expensive "private cremation," even though a former student has offered to dig a hole in your yard.

The vet tech tells you that your dog will be given something to calm her down, make her "loopy." You ask if you can have some. "Only if you want to puke," your vet says. "It makes dogs feel great, not so much with humans." Your dog very quickly stops dry heaving and foaming at the mouth. She lays her head down and seems to be in a very happy place. You pet her and talk to her and do your best not to cry because you do not want to upset her. Then the vet says she is giving the second injection. You keep your hand on your dog's chest, feel her heart slow and then stop.

You will not believe how easy the dying is. Afterward you wonder why we can't let our humans go in this way, with compassion and kindness and love.

"We'll be right back," your vet tells you. "Take a few minutes."

That is when you bury your face in the fur of your dead dog and wail. The vet and vet tech come back with a little stretcher; they will lift your dog onto it and cover her with a fuzzy ducky blanket that seems at once sentimental and silly but heartbreaking.

The next day you will relay your story to your running partner, Jen, and when you get to the ducky blanket, your voice cracks, and you have to stop talking. Jen says, "That isn't heartbreaking. It's soulbreaking."

And it was.

As with most dogs, Riva Jones taught me how to be a better creature in the world. How to live in the moment, to go with the flow. How to be a friend. How to live and, finally, how to let go.

Even though I wanted to prevent her from suffering even one single minute, I couldn't. The last twenty hours of her life were uncomfortable, really uncomfortable. But I have to believe Riva could see I did the best I could. Would it have been more humane to put her down a week earlier, when I had made the first appointment? Probably. But as it is, I still sometimes wonder if I should have brought her into the vet's office that morning to have the doctor check her. Maybe she'd be alive today! Those are the irrational thoughts that go along with the here-one-day, gone-the-next nature of death. I even worried Riva would "wake up" in the vet's office, scared, wondering where I was.

Everyone says your dog will tell you when it's time. That you will know. That only makes sense in retrospect. You did it, so it was very much the right time.

Craig didn't send me a check for half the euthanasia or cremation, but he did call me to tell me he would be coming up to Tahoe to spread Riva's ashes. When I told Tom, he said, "Tell him no cash, no ash."

I went back and forth about what to do. Finally, I opened the wooden box (a private cremation comes with a lovely cedar container), and we dished some of Riva into another baggie for Craig. As I did with my father's ashes, I sifted through Riva's remains, hoping for what, I'm not sure. Some feeling that it was her. But as with my father, it was gray bone fragment, and I could make no connection between it and the living being.

When I went to meet Craig with the ash and Riva's collar, he asked me if I wanted to go with him. I felt like I needed an ending to our story, an ending, in many ways, to my relationship with my ex. We had kept in close contact because of Riva, but that would be over now. I then realized that the day he sat on the deck with me, drinking chardonnay, he was there not so much to say goodbye to Riva as to say goodbye to me.

We hiked up the hill behind the house we once shared. Since her death, he had gotten a dog paw tattooed on his bicep and, underneath, Riva's name. I refrained from telling him, even in my usual passive-aggressive way, how ridiculous I found the tattoo. I saw that even though we had lost the same dog, we both had our own distinct journey with the loss. When we reached the top, the forested valley unfolding into the lake, Craig opened the baggie and let the wind take the ash. It swirled around, scattering on the dirt below us. He then drove a metal cross into the ground with a mallet and wrapped Riva's collar around it. We both sat there for a long time, looking out across the lake.

A woman with a dog came up the trail and said, "Great spot, huh?"

We allowed that it was.

"My husband proposed to me right there," she called. "Right where you're sitting."

She walked off with her dog, and I said, "Should we tell her?" We both laughed for a long time and then agreed it was time to head back down. When we reached my car, Craig gave me a check for half the vet bill without being asked.

And then, finally, we said goodbye.

Rites of Passage

My husband told me not to tell anyone about the five lesions inside his colon. I assured him I had only mentioned it to a couple of people because I was worried.

When we got the results, I texted my people to tell them Tom's polyps were benign. I was happy to share the good news with my friends. If the results had come back as cancer, they would have been the people I needed around me.

Until recently, I didn't know one of the rites of passage of middle age included a passage up the rear with a small camera on a wire. And people like my husband don't talk about these things; he is midwestern-nice, which means you don't bring up things like alcoholism, abortion, infidelity, and failed marriages. Unfortunately for him, he married a writer, and these are my top subjects. You also don't discuss my newest topic: colonoscopies and polyps.

When I admitted to him how many people I had told about his polyps, my usually calm husband became upset. "You didn't really tell twelve people," he said.

You know how your dog looks down and away when you come home to find shit on the carpet and ask, "Who did this?" Well, that's the tactic I used, the one that says, "Who me? I don't know who messed up the carpet. But can I have a treat?"

Tom said, "You can tell anyone what you want about you, but don't talk about me. You need to have some boundaries."

"But this was about me too," I said. "I was worried about you. Where's the boundary?"

"My body is a boundary," he said, and he pointed at himself, as if it might be unclear where I ended and he began.

My response to being told not to tell anyone something is to tell everyone, so I said to Tom, "Sure, okay."

But here's the thing: it feels like it's my business—the inside of my husband's butt—because I was with him all night while he sat on the toilet after drinking the super-laxative, and then I woke at the break of dawn to get him to the hospital. I waited there so I could drive his silly drugged-up ass home.

And because I'm the worrier in the family, when things were taking longer than I thought they should, I did what I do best: *imagine the worst.*

My growing concern was interrupted by an actual situation near the elevators. A woman—maybe someone who was also drugged and had escaped the colonoscopy assembly line—started screaming and yelling. I was afraid it was Tom, so I went to investigate. Just as I got there, a woman lifted her hospital gown and peed on the elevator floor. The doors closed on her, mid-pee. I went back to the couches in the nearby lobby, but I soon heard the Code Gray. I imagined the security guards descending on her somewhere on the floors below. Who knew there would be so much excitement in the butt-scoping ward?

Things quieted down, and my husband finally wheeled by. When he saw me in the waiting room, he gave a wistful little wave. I followed him into the curtained room. A hospital administrator soon came by to ask him if there was anything they could do to improve his experience. "As a matter of fact," he said, still under the influence of the fentanyl and midazolam cocktail, "You could warm up the lube before you put it up my ass."

She said there was nothing she could do about that. I wondered if she was bored at work and asked her patients questions while they were drugged to add a little pizzazz to her day. It wasn't a terrible strategy for a guaranteed laugh, and I thought about how some days at my job teaching freshman composition, I used similar strategies, though the students had drugged themselves.

Then the doctor, who had a tiny mustache, hair greased back to hide a bald spot, and a very long face—a man who looked exactly like someone who scoped buttholes all day—came in. He told us there were five polyps. He pointed to where they were on his own body. And then he said, "The trouble is they are flat."

"Flat?" I asked, thinking I had misheard him.

"Yes, they need to go to pathology. And if they're fine, we'll see you in another three years." With that he turned on the heel of his expensive shoes and disappeared behind the curtain. I made a joke about the Wizard of Ass and then did the thing you should only do if you want to scare the hell out of yourself: I googled.

I learned the flat things in my husband's colon were called sessile polyps. I also found out they are either precancer or else they are cancer. The doctor didn't tell us how big they were or what he thought, so I asked the nurse. She responded to me by handing me pictures of my husband's colon. The lesions looked like canker sores, and because of the magnification, they seemed giant.

Google told me the larger the sessile polyps were, the more likely they were cancerous. I asked the nurse, "How big are these?" She told us to ask the doctor, but he never reappeared.

I hadn't yet heard of anyone having polyps in the colon, but truth be told, I had never asked anyone either. The parts of our bodies that betray our animal natures and remind us of our animal bodies, the locations of procreation and excretion, are off-limit topics in polite conversation. We deny the most natural parts of ourselves—our hunger or desires, our vulnerabilities and frailties, and even our grief.

And maybe polyp talk is common after fifty. When I was young, I swore I'd never be one of those old people who talks about hot flashes or my colon—or in this case, my husband's colon. But then you find yourself middle-aged with not only hot flashes but rage flashes, too, which barrel down the track like a runaway train, and you can't help but mention it. When you think your car seat or, worse, your plane seat is on actual fire, it's hard not to say something, though in the case of the airplane, it might unsettle your seatmates. I know this from experience.

And so it goes with the colon, that five-foot-long miracle that reabsorbs water and micronutrients, stores waste, and is home to the trillions of bacteria making up our microbiome.

While we waited the ten days for the pathology to come back, I asked my friend Brenda if she had ever had a colonoscopy. "Oh yeah," she said. "I've had a couple."

"But you're only fifty-four. Why have you had more than one?"

"They found some stuff."

"Like what?"

"I don't know. But they took them off, and the next one was fine."

"Like polyps."

"I guess so," she said.

"Were they flat, or did they have stalks?" I asked and then added, "The ones with stalks look like little mushrooms." I was premed as an undergraduate, but now I had an MD in proctology (now known as colorectal surgery) from the University of Google.

Brenda told me she didn't know, and it was clear she didn't care whether the things in her colon looked like mushrooms or not. I don't understand people like this. I mean, if there's something blooming inside your colon, wouldn't you want to know what kind of vegetable it resembled? Nonetheless, I felt better, knowing someone else I knew had had polyps. I wondered why I never knew this before about Brenda but then realized not everyone tells her twelve closest friends about her polyps. My husband certainly didn't.

I continued my medical studies at Google University. I learned that 25 percent of all colonoscopies find polyps. I also learned there are different kinds, some carrying a higher risk of cancer than others. To my husband's chagrin, I also learned the staples of his diet—red meat and beer—contribute to them. But the doctor hadn't said a word to him about any of the risk factors, nor did he mention that vitamin D and calcium might help prevent them; this is something people under fifty should clearly know.

I then wrote to my former dissertation advisor (I ended up with a doctorate in literature, not medicine, which might be obvious by now). I knew she had had colon cancer but had never heard the details. She wrote back and told me to call her, so I did.

Like Brenda, she's a no-nonsense woman, and she said, "Even if it's cancer, it's no big deal. They just snip-snip-snip and you're fine. The only ill effect is if I eat a rich French dinner, I have diarrhea, but sometimes it's worth it, but that's probably too much information." I assured her that was *exactly* the kind of information I was after. "And besides," my advisor continued, "lots of people have polyps and they never turn into cancer."

I knew that many people died of colon cancer, but I preferred to hang onto every word my dissertation advisor had said, even if she, too, was an expert in Victorian literature and not medicine.

I told Tom that more than anything else, it was these conversations that allowed me not to panic while we waited for the results. "As long as you don't write about it," he said.

I looked up from the computer, at the beginnings of this very story, and I nodded.

But of course, years later, I told Tom I had written about him, and he said, "I don't like this at all. It makes you sound like an asshole for not caring what I think."

I laughed, "Asshole! That's funny," but Tom didn't laugh, so I asked, "What would you like me to do about it?" I didn't tell him I didn't care if I sound like an asshole because sometimes I *am* an asshole. He already knows that.

"I don't know," he said. "It's your story. Write another few sentences showing I've read it and am fine with you writing it."

"Aren't you due for another colonoscopy soon?" I asked. "Maybe that will give me more material, something more to say about you and your butt?"

"You really are an asshole," Tom said. This time we both laughed.

And when Tom's next colonoscopy came around, he would not allow me to come into the hospital with him.

Traveling with the Dead

Egrets land on raised coffins in the rice paddies. Women wearing straw hats sell sodas on the side of the road. We have booked a boat called *The Bassaic*, run by a French company, to ferry us down the Mekong. The crew keeps us separate from the French.

We wait for the only other English-speaking tourists to load the boat. The husband has swoopy hair and square-framed sunglasses. He helps the wife on, who spills onto the boat in a flash of gold and neon pink—a hot-pink halter top, ripped designer jeans, gold tennis shoes with gold ribbon laces tied into bows. She could easily fold her tiny body into her giant suitcase and disappear into it if she wanted. The man refuses to hand over their passports to the crew. They both decline to drink the juice. They speak Spanish, and I hear the husband say, looking toward me and my husband, "Americans." There is disdain in his voice.

I hadn't said it aloud, but before they boarded and I heard them speak, I thought the same about them.

The wife disappears in her cabin and then remerges for lunch, wearing a tight, backless black dress. We eat lunch, and when the dessert comes—a rice pancake with fried banana and dark chocolate—I eat with glee, even if my belly pushes against my pants. The wife rebuffs the dessert, asks the waiter, "Do you want me fat?" The waiter shrugs.

I know that to look like she does, it means denying yourself the best dessert ever, even on vacation. It makes me want to eat more, but I know I can't say I will have hers.

We are kept separate from the French the entire time—like Brexit, I joke. We share the deck with the Spanish-speaking couple, but they also speak English.

I speak to them in Spanish. I tell them we're from California, as if that excuses us from being American. They tell us they are from Panama. "Not Florida," the husband says, "the country." I say I understand and that we have been to Panama, the country. I tell them we hate our new president, the former television reality show conman.

The French complain because we have the upstairs deck while they are below. The husband from Panama, Andrus, tells the crew we will switch for dinner. I tell Andrus I can't imagine demanding other people get moved for the betterment of my experience. The wife—Gabriela—agrees. We all become friends.

We pass the French briefly on the metal stairs. The deck below is shady, giving us a break from the southern sun.

We watch the sunrise together the next morning—a pink orb in the smoky sky. The red flag whips at the back of the boat, the yellow star appearing and disappearing in the wind. A fan rustles the tinsel of a fake Christmas tree. We share lychee, plums, rambutan, and oranges. Gabriela says she can't eat the durian. I eat her portion. Andrus says he agrees with the new president's Muslim ban. I explain, conjuring my smartest and most measured voice, why I disagree. Gabriela looks me in the eye and says, "I agree with you."

We walk through villages that evening. Insects hum in the yellow glow. Caged roosters and dogs chirp and bark. Gabriela asks, "You're a teacher, right?" I nod. She says, "I am nothing. I'm just a mom."

I tell her being a mom is an important job, and I mean it. "And I bet you're a good mom," I say, and she smiles. I look out across the Mekong River, and I think about my own mother.

We board a smaller wooden boat, churn through the brown-green water, weave through the maze of floating markets—tire-lined boats full of pineapple, jackfruit, squash, watermelon, cabbage. Plastic-covered houses with tin roofs on stilts line the river's banks. Gabriela carries a Coach purse. She says, "The poor here are worse off than in Panama. They have nothing. No hope." I want to say we can't speak for them but say nothing. Because what do I know? Only two days earlier I would not have guessed how much I would enjoy the company of this slick couple—I am taught the same lesson again and again: people are more than they initially seem to be.

We kiss Andrus and Gabriela goodbye on each cheek, head for our Can Tho hotel, twelve stories of green glass and neon lights. A whirl of motorbikes zooms past. A dancing pineapple tries to lure us into a bar. Plucked chickens, with their necks broken, hang in street-side stalls. Their beaks akimbo. Their half-open eyes gaze back at us through the smudged glass. What did the heads see when their bodies darted in the yard? A grassy knoll, the triangle of blue sky, a wire cage.

That night I can't sleep, walk to the floor-to-ceiling windows, press my palms against the glass, the dark night; the river cruise topped by a giant neon lotus chugs through the black water below. I think about my mother again. This is the first international trip we have taken since she died six months ago. So far from home, and yet she is right here. And I am here—traveling with the dead, the memories run like a film reel, catching. "You're a good mom," I told her near the end.

She said, "Stop acting like I'm dying."

Saying the things you should say is admitting to the end. And maybe Mother knew her life held more meaning if she stayed in denial, for how much is the life of the dying worth? Being a mother is an important job, one she wasn't about to quit just yet.

We are up early the next day for a bicycle tour of the Mekong Delta. We are given rickety bikes. I ask for a helmet and am met with a blank stare.

We follow narrow paths though banana, mango, and durian trees, up and over wooden bridges. We swerve out of the way of motorbikes, and I wish I were wearing a helmet. We ride ferries across waterways, motorcycles revving their engines in anticipation for the other side.

Our guide leads us to a sacred grove. He lights incense and prays. We are told the many-rooted bodhi trees are sacred. I walk away from the rest of the group. A breeze slices through the humid air. I see her again from the corner of my eye. She disappears when I look for her straight-on. The way it always was. I mouth the words now: *You're a good mom.*

Even here, in the hot and humid breeze a world away, I hear her say it: *Stop acting like I'm dying.*

These bodies die, but we spend much of our time pretending otherwise. We are too far from death until we are too close. Then we have no way to talk about it.

We fly over the South China Sea, travel to a Vietnamese-owned luxury resort. The hotel is newly opened, taking marketing photographs—the models, a tall, handsome Western man walking with a petite Vietnamese woman.

We walk the beaches until our feet are black with tar. I ask for turpentine in the lobby.

In the morning we watch as hotel employees clean the beach. My husband says, "Top ten things you will find on the beaches of Con Dao," making fun of the bucket lists in travel magazines, the kinds of things I sometimes write for money.

"Hypodermic needles, that's number one for sure," I say. "Plastic sandals are number two."

We head to the other side of the island, tour the Con Dao prison, where shackled clay mannequins occupy old cells. They wear scowls, looks of despair: the reenactment of torture. Starved, naked bodies in the tiger cages. Human bodies, made animal. Light casts barred shadows on the cement walls. I enter the cells, and one makes me feel so nauseated I must leave immediately. I wonder if it's the banh mi we ate on the street in front of the museum, but once I am back in the humid air, I feel better. I remind myself to accept the mysterious, haunted world behind the world and the limits of my own understanding.

I hear a British man say, "America has had so many puppets." I want to say the French built these prisons. I want to ask him where he thinks we came from, whose puppets we were, how we learned imperialism and colonialism so very well. I want to say that though the British stayed out of this particular war, they have done their share of holding the strings.

On this trip I've learned to say, "the American War." I have learned people and things are more than what they might seem. I have learned traveling means witnessing the world exactly as it is without trying to change it and to let my travels change me instead. I have learned how to travel with my dead.

There are cages enough everywhere.

The Disappearing Act

I.

Your friend Brenda used to say, "You can't rape the willing." It always bothered you, but like many things she said, you let it slide. You didn't say there's a difference between will and desire. You didn't say the words *rape* and *willing* do not belong in the same sentence, especially not in that way she had arranged them. You didn't ask what happens when the willing changes her mind or drinks too much to remember.

2.

Once when you were teaching a creative writing class and you asked students what they wanted to write about, one of the students, Liv, shouted, "Blackout sex." You wrote that on the board, along with "my grandmother" and "hiking the Appalachian Trail." The room went quiet for a while. It was the first day of class. Liv turned out to be the strongest writer.

3.

When you were a junior in college, you lived in a houseful of women on Ramona Drive. You took turns sharing bedrooms and having your own. This was during one of the times you had your own room. This thing that happened, the one you still can't remember.

4.

You woke up next to someone you knew, not a friend exactly. Someone who sat nearby in a class maybe. Or one of the guys in the fraternity next door. You don't remember that either.

5.

He was dark haired, with large close-set eyes and a hairless chest. He was handsome, though you hadn't liked him in that way, or at least that's how you remember it. You woke up naked in your bed. You asked him what happened. He said, "You don't remember?" You told him you didn't. He said that nothing happened, that you just passed out there together. In your bed.

6.

You knew it wasn't true, that nothing had happened. And in another version of the same memory, he said that if you didn't remember, you should do it again. You don't know if he actually said this. Then he dressed very quickly, pulling on shorts and a shirt, and left. You later found his underwear. Black briefs tangled in your sheets. You thought about washing and returning them.

7.

You tell yourself you wanted only to blur the boundaries of yourself, not obliterate them. But it isn't the allure of the siren's song but the crashing surf on rocks, the splintering. Because isn't it true that when you look over the precipice, you realize all you ever wanted was to throw yourself into it? Disappearing altogether is your magic trick.

8.

This was back when you only called it rape if a stranger jumped out of the bushes.

9.

Even when this happened to your friend, the stranger in the night, she didn't go to the police. She begged you to tell no one. Hadn't her skirt been too short? What was she doing drunk, walking home alone from a party? She sat on your twin bed, her head leaned back against the concrete dorm wall, and she cried. You could see her red-soaked panties. How could any of you have suggested she tell someone, make it all the worse for her?

10.

And hadn't the fact that the large-eyed boy was in your house and your room and your bed proved you had been willing? Because you couldn't remember, you had always believed you had been the one to betray yourself. *You can't rape the willing.* And because you can't remember, you have always called this another near-miss. Even if bruises bloomed on your inner thighs like blue flowers.

Honky-Tonk Woman

A group of men followed us down Broadway, the bustling honky-tonk district in Nashville, Music City, USA. They shouted to us: "Ladies, ladies, LAAADDDIIIIEES."

Wendy and I stopped on the street corner and asked what they wanted. Neon signs flashed above: *Broadway Brewhouse, Betty Boots, AJ's Good Time Bar.* On the street a drummer beat on a plastic bucket, hoping for tips. A sleeping man in army fatigues curled up next to a pit bull, who wore a little army hat of his own.

"Hey ladies, where's the best music?"

"We aren't locals," Wendy said. "We are friends from college on a road trip together."

"Like Thelma and Louise," I said, "but we're driving a rented Toyota Corolla and not a 1966 Thunderbird."

The older man—the one who turned out to be the dad—laughed. The other men, who were really still boys, looked at me with blank faces, oblivious to the film reference. The dad asked, "Where are you ladies from?"

We told them California, and they told us they were from Georgia, these five young men and a dad, who had taken the group of friends to Nashville to celebrate his son's twenty-first birthday. We thought this was sweet, so we forgave the way they had shouted at us. The dad was about our age, late forties, and looked like he could have stepped out of a Lands' End catalog. The boys seemed the typical preppy university types.

Since I had been in Alabama all month at a writing residency, I had started asking locals what they thought about the recent abortion ban there. I asked the grocery store clerks, Lyft drivers, even people on the street, so I asked these men about Georgia's abortion ban, also known by supporters as the "six-week heartbeat" law, even though a fetus doesn't technically have a functioning heart until twenty-two weeks.

"I'm for the new law," the dad said. "A heartbeat's a heartbeat. A life."

"Even in cases of rape or incest?" I asked. "What about that?"

"It isn't the baby's fault," he said.

While I discussed the recent abortion laws with the dad and one of the young men, Wendy talked to two of the other young men. I couldn't hear their discussion because of the honky-tonk music. The boy who was turning twenty-one and another friend wandered off to go to another bar, perhaps embarrassed by the dad, who acted like the very loud leader of the pack.

"My mother nearly aborted me," the dad said and pointed to himself as if I might not get his meaning. He said, "Conception means life, that is, if you believe in God."

"That's an either-or logical fallacy," I said. "And what about all the leftover embryos from IVF? Is it wrong to destroy those too?"

"I've never thought about that before," he said, shaking his head. The traffic light turned green, and an anxious driver blared his horn.

"According to your definition of human life, those are lives too," I pointed out. Three young women in strappy sundresses stumbled past.

"I'll have to think about that," the dad said and rested his chin between his thumb and finger. Then he pulled his hand away from his face, pointed to the sky, and said, "I always think about what Jesus would do."

"Just make sure you aren't creating God in your own image," I said. The scantily dressed cowgirl on the Nudie's Honky Tonk neon sign flashed above us, her lithe body in blue, her long hair in pale yellow.

The dad shook his head and said, "Of course not," and then without missing a beat, he asked, "Are you married?"

"Happily," I said.

"I'm happily married too. I've got a great wife. I probably don't deserve her."

I nodded. It seemed as though we had found a point of agreement.

The son's friend told me if a woman takes enough vitamin C, she can self-abort: "I bet you didn't know that vitamin C heats up the uterus and the baby will die," he said.

"I was not aware of such a fact," I said.

He went on, telling me he had an infant son, and though he didn't get to see him much, he loved him just the same. He shouted, pointing at my face with his long index finger: "She tried to kill the baby with vitamin C." Then he added, more quietly, "But it didn't work, thank God."

"I'm not surprised." I was beginning to feel like Allen Funt would jump out from a nearby honky-tonk, shouting, "Smile! You're on *Candid Camera!*"

But this was no joke. These men, affluent and educated, were the prototype of those who currently controlled women's bodies with a dangerous combination of privilege and ignorance.

People pushed by us on the street corner, dark shadows against the flashing neon lights in the shape of cowboy boots, lassos, and the scantily clad cowgirl straddling a guitar.

"I don't personally know anyone who's had an abortion," the dad said. "But I'm sure those women regret their decision."

I laughed, and he asked, "What's so funny?"

"Trust me. You know women who have had abortions, but they aren't going to tell you."

"I don't know anyone who's had an abortion," he repeated.

"One in four women have had an abortion. But women are shamed into keeping it a secret."

"I don't know any women like that," he said.

"Well you know me. I'm one of those women, and you know what? I don't regret it." For the first time in our conversation, he stopped talking over me, so I went on: "I regret having to make the decision in the first place. But the decision? It was one of the best decisions in my life."

"I'm sorry," he said and put his hand on my shoulder. He looked at me in that way so many other men had looked at me right before they were about to lean in and kiss me, the eyes focused and slit, all lid and iris and lens.

I froze. He leaned in to kiss my forehead—an act both predatory and patronizing. I wriggled my shoulder away from his hand and flung my arm up to stop him. He grabbed my wrist and kissed my hand. He was a man handsome enough that he had probably gotten away with this kind of behavior his entire life.

I knew I had to get out of there. I pulled my hand away from him and signaled to Wendy it was time to go. We started walking away, but they followed us, the dad restarting his loop about how his life had nearly been aborted, and that's when I turned around and said, "Maybe she should have."

He stopped when this registered, and he asked, "Should have what?"

"Should have had the abortion," I said. By this point I wanted to end the conversation with Mr. Lands' End, to be rid of him, and I thought that would do it.

He put his hand over his heart and said, "I'm a wonderful person with an amazing wife. I have great kids. All that would be gone."

"The world would have been fine without you and your children." I turned back around, grabbed Wendy's hand, and we hurried down the busy sidewalk. We weaved past party revelers and beggars and jaywalked across the street. I turned around again, and they were still behind us, so we quickened our pace. I told Wendy, "Louise shot that guy for a reason."

Drunks and live country music poured onto the streets. Neon flashed in the storefronts, and a U.S. flag flapped in the hot wind. Wendy told me how the young man she was talking to kept telling her how pretty she was and begged to kiss her. Wendy is tall and thin with long blonde hair, blue eyes, and model cheekbones, but she was more than twice this boy's age. He looked like a friend her teenaged daughter might bring home. She's also married, which she explained, but then he asked, "But are you *happily* married?"

Wendy told me she offered the young man career counseling instead of a kiss, and she urged him not to take over his father's dentistry practice. "I asked him what makes him happy," she said. "And his answer was money. He said money was the only thing that makes him happy."

We crossed the street on a crowded crosswalk, and the men followed. I thought they'd eventually give up, but the dad started calling to us again: "Ladies! Where are you going?"

We picked up our pace, then steered into AJ's Good Time Bar. They pursued us. We made a quick U-turn out of the bar, and so did they. Now at a jog, we retraced our steps down the busy sidewalk. The dad kept trying to get our attention. "California!" he shouted, because we hadn't revealed our names, only where we were from. "Let me buy you a drink."

I shouted back, "Go away."

"But I want to keep talking to you, California."

We passed the Axe Throwing Game Room, then ducked into Nudie's Honky Tonk. Only the dad trailed us now. The band played bluegrass, and we weaved through the dancing patrons, across the beer-sticky floors. The fiddle played a solo, and dancers of all ages swayed hips and waved tattooed arms overhead. Women shook their short denim skirts or twirled long, flowing dresses; men, wearing backward baseball caps or cowboy hats, nodded in time to the beat. I wanted to dance, continuing the fun times with my college girlfriend, but the dad stalked me through the crowd. I ran down the stairs and into the ladies' room—a place I knew he wouldn't follow me.

When Wendy found me there near the sink, she said, "I took care of it. He's gone."

"I'm sorry I ran away. All of a sudden fight-or-flight took over. How did you get him to leave?" Women came and went, checking their images in the mirror, applying lip gloss and fixing their hair.

Wendy lathered her hands with soap, scrubbing them with an unusual vigor. "I told him you were done with him, and he needed to leave us alone." She put one soapy hand in the air, showing me the gesture she'd used, and said, "She's done."

"What did he say?"

"He kissed my hand," Wendy said, making a face in the mirror. She rinsed her hands and pulled a paper towel from the dispenser. "But I got rid of him and then washed him away." She dried her hands with the paper towel and then tossed it into the trash.

"Thank you," I said. "I would hate to have to end our story by driving off a cliff."

"No," Wendy laughed. "Let's call a Lyft instead."

Auntie Suzanne

"Auntie Soo-Zaaannn," Luke called from the downstairs bathroom.

"He wants you to wipe his butt," Kristin told me. She continued to work on her laptop.

"Yeah, right," I said.

"Sooo-Zaaannn."

"He does," she said. "You'd better go down there."

I walked down the stairs, not really expecting to find Luke in need of ass wiping, but sure enough, he was sitting on the toilet, his ear-to-ear grin like a watermelon rind.

"Wipe me," he said.

"No way."

"I want you to wipe me."

"Auntie Suzanne doesn't do butts."

When Luke and I came up the stairs together, Kristin asked, "Did you wipe him?"

"No. I supervised. Dry, wet, dry. I'm sure it's fine."

Luke scratched at his itchy butt.

Kristin and her three children, a three-year-old boy and two six-year-old girls, had come to visit. She had a conference at Harveys Casino, and it was my job to teach the children to ski while she worked. It had snowed six feet in three days. The fair-weather children had no interest in being outdoors at all, even though I had purchased a couple of plastic sleds for them, so I had to plan for some indoor fun instead.

With a boxful of Burning Man clothes, crayons and coloring sheets, and books, I felt ready to entertain three children for a couple of days.

The costume fun, coloring, and book reading lasted all of about two hours, not two days. I was doomed. Plus, the snow was so good I kept looking out the window with longing.

Because I had run out of things to do, I took the children to get pedicures. I had scoffed at a friend who had taken her five-year-old daughter to get a pedicure, saying, "I was thirty before my first pedicure." Now pedicures for children seemed like a reasonable idea. I had to get them out of the house, away from my furniture, which they jumped all over, and the dog, who kept trying to bite Luke.

I have to come clean here. I wasn't left entirely alone with the children, thank God, because none of us would have survived. Kristin brought her Brazilian au pair along. And still, I couldn't do it, even with a nanny. Most days I look at the clock, lamenting how fast time moves. For those two days I willed the clock to tick to five o'clock, which was when I allowed myself my first caipirinha, the national drink of Brazil (the nanny did come in handy, but for three children I needed three nannies, maybe four). Drinking took off the proverbial edge, and I could see how nap time could become the new happy hour.

Although the kids wanted to play with Auntie Suzanne, the second morning I snuck out of the house before anyone noticed. I grabbed my skis and fled the children for new snow. As the chairlift whisked me up the mountain, I felt the frenzy of screaming children, with all their "I want, I want, I wants," start to fade.

"But don't you ski every day?" Kristin asked. "Can't you miss a few days?"

"Yes, but not every day is a powder day." It's pointless to explain this to a nonskier. The old saying "No friends on a powder day" isn't meant as ironic. I have spent my entire adult life living in the mountains, so when the perfect powder days arrive, I'll be ready. I wasn't about to let a pack of wild children keep me from fresh snow. The only parallels I can think of are the day of perfect waves for a surfer; the still, glass-like lake for the water-skier, kayaker, or paddleboarder; or the morning after a light rain, creating a kind of "brown powder" on the trails for a mountain biker. And it seems to me that these sorts of days come more often than the perfect powder day for skiers.

In the parking lot that morning, four teenaged snowboarders blasted something they referred to as "death metal" from their truck speakers. I retaliated by turning up the volume on a song I don't even like, Big Mountain's "Baby, I Love Your Way." They took their bong hits, picked up their boards, and lumbered toward the resort.

On my last run of the morning, I loaded onto a lift with another snowboarder, one just slightly older than the death metal fans. We both sat in silence, staring ahead into the storm. Two singles on a double. The chairlift swayed in the wind; the cloud-knitted skies spit snow onto our goggles. He chair danced to the music blasting from his iPod for a while, then took off his glove, fidgeted in his pocket, fished out a cigarette. His long blond hair stuck out from beneath his helmet.

He flicked his lighter again and again until he finally achieved a blue-orange flame and was able to light the cigarette. He took a deep inhale and said, "Fuckin' ay right." A thin trail of smoke twisted into the air.

"In the 1960s," I said to my young chairlift partner, "the writer Flannery O'Connor said we are a nation who has lost our manners. Do you find that truer than ever?" The snow pelted my cheeks. I wiped off my goggles with the back of my glove.

He couldn't hear me over his music. He continued chair dancing, flicking the accumulating snow from his snowboard. And smoking.

I stared ahead, into the storm, willing the chair to move faster.

He pulled one of the buds from his ear and turned to me, cigarette in his bare hand, and asked, "You know what?"

I shook my head.

"If you really want to cruise the pow-pow," he said, making a wavelike motion with the gloved hand, "you should try James Brown." He then made a curving motion with his other hand, the ashy tip of the cigarette flaking into the gray air.

"I should?"

"Fuckin' ay you should." He pointed at me, as if he didn't want me to think he might be addressing someone else. "He's the Father of Funk. Mr. Dy-na-mite!"

"And the godfather of soul."

"Abso-fucking-lutely," he said. "See, you know!" He gave me a thumbs-up, and I nodded, thinking we had finished our chit-chatting; then he said, "I, like, have to get back to work, man. I'm a lifty, but I'm on a ride break. But I'll tell you what. I'm gettin' some pow-pow now."

"Pow-pow with James Brown," I said, in a way I hoped sounded ironic.

"Affirmative." He smiled without a hint of irony. He put the bud back into his ear and resumed chair dancing. He then put out the cigarette, squirreled it back into his pocket, and put his glove back on. I noted this evidence of manners—not littering.

The pines bent with the wind. Wispy snow devils whirled below us. I couldn't help but think we belonged to not only different genders and generations but different species.

Or somehow, without noticing it, I had become very old—old enough, I realized in horror, to be this young man's mother.

At the top of the lift he said, "Get some, dude."

"You too," I called, skiing away, "with James Brown."

He gave me a gloved thumbs-up again and rode away, back toward his lift.

I dropped down The Face, kneeling into gravity, carving through storm. Low clouds obscured Lake Tahoe, so the earth and sky blended into a white net. I skied through the flat light, ducking into the trees.

I had thought about having my own children but always in the abstract, never really picturing the loud, messy, demanding little people they actually are. Planning for them always came down to how I could get pregnant without missing a ski season. And as I realized on the chairlift, I was already an old woman with even older eggs, made back when I myself was a fetus. It took me a long time to find the right man, and soon after we married, he announced one night at the dinner table he would like to "start a family."

I choked on my wine and asked, "Do you know how old I am?"

"You're forty."

"Do you know what the chances of a forty-year-old woman getting pregnant are?"

"You're healthy," Tom said.

I went to my gynecologist and had my hormones tested. All that skiing and trail running did not change the fact that I had a forty-year-old body complete with forty-year-old eggs, forty-one if you count gestation. The tests showed menopause was not far away. Coupled with a fibroid tumor and some ovarian cysts, it seemed I was not a very good candidate for pregnancy—far worse, in fact, than the average forty-year-old woman.

"I know you don't have a crystal ball," I said to the doctor, "but if you had to say what my chances are of getting pregnant, what do you think they would be? Ten percent?"

I could see her stiffen, perhaps ready for the tears. She said, "I would say less than one percent."

"Well, that's a relief!" My reaction surprised both me and my doctor. My new husband and I hadn't been using birth control, and we had bought a house that would easily accommodate another couple of humans. I thought I was ready for children. But in truth I wasn't sure what I had wanted. I didn't want to find myself with regrets later on, and I didn't know anyone who regretted *having* children, or at least *admitted* to regretting it. But it seemed to me the only thing in life you can't undo (aside from murder maybe) is having a baby, yet many people do it without much thought.

At the same time, for women there's a window of opportunity, and once you miss it, you either have to forget it or pay the thousands of dollars to endure the physical and emotional rockiness of in vitro fertilization. Tom and I both agreed no fertility specialists, no invasive procedures. If we had missed the proverbial boat, then so be it.

And here I was, being told my "ship had sailed."

I sometimes don't know how I feel until I'm really faced with a thing, and having the doctor, with her white coat and degrees framed on the wall behind her, say I would not be having children made it seem official. I felt relief without the hint of sadness I'd expected.

"This is usually a much more difficult conversation," the doctor said and sat back in her chair. "Many women are baby obsessed, and all of this can be quite upsetting."

When I returned home, I relayed the odds—less than 1 per-cent—to my husband.

"But not impossible," Tom said.

"I guess not impossible," I said. "But unlikely, like really unlikely."

"I guess we'll have to wrap our minds around that," he said.

"Yeah, I guess we will."

He looked at me and said, "Seems like you already have."

I agreed. I didn't think there was any sense in forcing my body to do something it didn't want to do. I could see how this could lead to an obsession, all based on thinking I wanted something because I couldn't have it, or at least not have it easily. By letting go of the idea of children right away, something in me knew I was saving myself from a whole lot of heartbreak. I haven't always been able to let go of things I can't change, but thank-fully, this was one time where I could. Or maybe I never wanted children in the first place, but as a woman, I had been taught that motherhood was something I was supposed to want and admitting that I didn't want children made me a bad woman.

Some mommies I know have told me there's no way to really know love until you have a child, but the love they describe is fueled by hormones, a sense of wonder because their bodies produced a tiny human, and the biological instinct to protect said tiny person. And maybe that's the definition of love. Or maybe those of us who have remained childless distribute our bounty of love farther, to our many friends and their children. And I make a great aunt—I finally did teach all of Kristin's children to ski, which everyone knows is Auntie Suzanne's specialty, or, some might say, obsession.

Also, there is this: there's nothing quite like being alone with your thoughts, skiing through lodgepole pines in the muffled silence of snowfall and that certain slant of morning light, maybe even humming "I Got You" as you give yourself fully to gravity.

The Danger Scale

Avalanche danger is determined by the likelihood, size, and distribution of avalanches.

Low Avalanche Danger: Generally safe avalanche conditions. Watch for unstable snow on isolated terrain features.

We thought we'd entered a cloud of snow crystals. Everything went white, like flying through a cloud in an airplane. Tiny slivers of ice fell around us and stuck to the fine hairs on my face, crusted onto my goggles, formed white debris on my jacket and ski pants. The chairlift in front of us disappeared into the white haze, as if we were inside a snow globe someone had given a rigorous shake. We stopped talking, wondering at this strange white fog swirling around us.

The night before, more than five feet of fresh snow had fallen. Pine trees sagged under the weight of new snow, the mountainscape obscured by the piles of white on white. Four of us were packed on the chairlift, heading up the mountain; we had been giddy all morning, skiing the fresh powder. Someone said, "Aren't we lucky to have such good friends to enjoy all this new snow with?" But I stiffened, my back against the cold metal, knowing Brenda would latch onto it.

"I never forget when someone is mean to me. That I never forget." Brenda looked in my direction and said, "I've never been a teacher."

No one responded to this strange non sequitur, but I knew what she meant.

That's when we entered the cloud and everything went white and eerie, cold and quiet.

We skied off the lift, and our friends who had been a few chairs ahead of us were waiting at the top. We skied to them, and one of our friends said, "I saw a snowboarder below the lift disappear in a wave of snow. He was there below us, and then he was gone. Who should I tell?" We told her to tell the lift attendant, and we would go to the bottom and start looking for our other friends. What if they had been skiing that run too?

We started skiing down, and I heard the whine and bark of the rescue dogs. I stopped, caught my breath, and said, "Oh shit." I started down again, and when we reached the bottom, we took out our phones and tried texting and calling our friends. Sirens echoed as ambulances and fire engines raced to the scene. Yellow CLOSED signs stretched across the lift line mazes. Skiers and snowboarders searched the parking lots for their friends and families. We were on our annual all-women's ski trip. Only half of our forty friends were accounted for. A uniformed man who was holding a radio told us to leave immediately: the mountain was shutting down; he wouldn't tell us why, though we already knew. The fog we had traveled through and the white wave that had engulfed the snowboarder was the powder cloud from an in-bounds avalanche.

We found out later a large swath had broken from the top of the mountain and a river of snow slid down the run Climax and funneled into Upper Dry Creek, a narrow chute, before stopping at the base of chair 5. The slide had partially buried two snowboarders our friend had seen disappear under the lift and a couple of the lift operators who were digging out the chairlift below.

The lines for the buses snaked around the frozen parking lot. The roads were snow covered, so we skied the mile or so back to the condo. Vehicles spun out on the icy roads; I wondered if we would be hit by a skidding car or truck. It's illegal to ski on the highway, but we didn't know that at the time. Also, we didn't know how else to get back to the condo. The gravel thrown onto the icy road made a grating sound as I pushed and skated and slid along the icy roads.

Brenda hadn't been speaking to me, aside from small digs like the one on the chairlift. That morning she had told me she and Christine had cleaned all the snow off the car while I was putting on makeup. I didn't think it would do any good to tell her I wasn't wearing any makeup, so I said, "I'm sorry you feel that way."

She said, "Christine is *helpful*."

"You can't compare me to Christine."

Brenda asked me why not, and I said, "Because Christine is the most helpful person on the planet. That's not even fair; no one is helpful in comparison." And I knew this wasn't about the snow on the car or whether or not I was helpful. This was about the night before, when a bunch of us were soaking in the hot tub at the condo. Huge flakes of snow fell into our hair, onto our steamy arms, into the water, where they dissolved. Our backs were against the jets, faces clouded by steam. We were drinking rosé out of plastic wine glasses and were happy after a day of powder skiing at Mammoth Mountain and the promise of more untracked snow to come. Someone—a fellow teacher—said something about how the current president wanted to arm teachers in response to recent school shootings.

"That's the most ridiculous thing I have ever heard," I said.

"I think we *should* arm teachers," Brenda said.

Another teacher, one who worked at the local high school, said, "Yeah right. Can you see me armed with a gun at school?"

Brenda said she could. "It's a good idea." She reached her arms up onto the concrete ledge and leaned back.

Brenda had grown up with guns; she had a small pink pistol "for protection," the one I asked her if I could borrow in the middle of the night to shoot my dying dog. Even if she hadn't said no, I wouldn't have been able to go through with it, of course, but I was desperate because, like so many pet owners, I had waited too long and I wanted to end my dog's pain.

I pulled away from my hot tub jet, sat up, and asked Brenda, "What?" even though I knew what. This wasn't the first time we disagreed about politics, and the divide had deepened since the last election, but I had had a couple glasses of wine and I was tired of having to stifle my opinions around her, so I said, "It's a terrible idea. We need fewer guns, not more guns. More guns are not the answer."

Brenda wasn't backing down. "Well, I think we should arm teachers."

"Can you imagine what kind of environment that would create in the classroom?" I asked.

"A safer one," Brenda said.

"You've never been a teacher," I said.

Brenda got out of the hot tub, grabbed her towel, and walked away.

Though she might not have taught full-time in the classroom like I did, Brenda spent her life teaching in one way or another. She taught skiing for years, and for a short spell she substituted in elementary school classrooms, which I had forgotten about until now.

But this wasn't why she was so angry. I wasn't supposed to "talk politics" in front of her: that's the invisible line I had crossed, the terrain trap I had willfully entered.

Moderate Avalanche Danger: Heightened avalanche conditions on specific terrain features. Evaluate snow and terrain carefully; identify features of concern.

Mother had told me, "You mustn't let that man break up your friendship."

I liked that she referred to the president by "that man" and not his name. "I don't see how I can be friends with someone who voted for him."

"Brenda's been a good friend to you. You break up your friendship with her, and you let him win."

"*That man's* main appeal is white supremacy. That's a deal breaker," I said.

"She's been a very good friend to you. Think about what you're giving up."

We had started Mother's chemotherapy the day before. Her second day of chemo fell on election day, and I wore a pantsuit to the doctor's office in support of my candidate. That night, with mother's body full of poison and lung cancer, we watched the election returns. The champagne I had bought sat unopened in the refrigerator. Mother and I argued. I went to bed before the official announcement came in because I saw it coming and couldn't stomach it. Mother and I had to be back at the doctor's office early the next morning for her third day of chemotherapy. I was losing my person, my mother, but also, now I was losing a country, or at least that's how it felt.

My mother had left England, become an American citizen— she always said she did this for me. That's one of the things she had gifted me—a whole new country.

I told Mother I couldn't believe anyone would vote for him. When I found out Brenda had voted for him, I asked her why.

"I'm tired of politicians. I went for the rogue businessman," she said. "Hopefully, it will work out."

"He's a reality TV show host. He's not even a good business-man," I said.

"We'll see," Brenda had said. And then she asked me if this was a mountain I was willing to die on, meaning if I kept talking, it might be the death of our friendship. She changed the subject, and I went along with the diversion.

I later told my friend Camille I couldn't believe he got in. She wasn't surprised, that this was the America she had known all along. She didn't tell me I was naive, but I knew I was. Camille is Black, and I am white, and that fact is important and informs both her knowledge and my ignorance. When I asked Camille about my friendship with Brenda, she said, "I wouldn't be friends with a Ku Klux Klan member."

When I told Mother this, she said, "Brenda isn't in the KKK, is she?"

I told her I didn't think she was. "But still."

"Still what?" Mother asked, aiming her remote at the television. "She has been a good friend to you."

Considerable Avalanche Danger: Dangerous avalanche conditions. Careful snowpack evaluation, cautious route-finding and conservative decision-making are essential.

Brenda is the kind of person who keeps her word. If she says she is going to fly across the world and meet you, she'll do it. And once she gets there, she will be an intrepid, up-for-anything travel partner, whether you are backpacking in a rainstorm, touring haunted wine caves, or skiing an icy chute.

She had been there for me when I finally left my first husband for good; when my favorite dog, Riva, died; and when I spread my father's ashes at the top of Mammoth Mountain's chair 23 on the twentieth anniversary of his death. But more than anything else, Brenda flew to Southern California to come help me when my mother died; I was alone, and she came and spent a week helping me sort through my mother's things. Before she arrived, the route-finding was hopeless: I walked around my mother's house in circles, touching her things, my knees buckling until I fell onto the wood floors and wept.

Brenda arrived and gave me direction. She sorted and cleaned and called all the right people. She knew which of my mother's items were valuable enough to sell and which should be donated. She made lists for me and handed me a pen and told me to cross off each item once I was finished. She put food and water and wine in front of me. Without her I wouldn't have remembered to eat. I didn't have to think. I only had to follow her no-nonsense directions. I was my mother's only daughter, and I couldn't have done this impossible thing without Brenda.

High Avalanche Danger: Very dangerous avalanche conditions. Travel in avalanche terrain not recommended.

Brenda and I met for a walk in the woods behind my house. We had spoken very little since that trip to Mammoth, the weekend of the avalanche.

First, we spoke of small, insignificant things. What we had been doing lately, how her parents were, what our sisters were up to. We started uphill along the creek, and she said, "I have a lot of liberal friends, and you're the only one I have trouble with. Why is that?"

I followed her, so I spoke to her back, told her I wasn't sure, asked her why she thought so.

"I don't know." She started to breathe heavily on the uphill, so her answers were short. And then she told me again how I wasn't helpful enough on the Mammoth ski trip. How I didn't help dig out the car or carry any of the heavy things up the stairs to the condo. How I didn't take a turn driving her beast of a car.

I told her I was sorry, but I also said, "I told you I would drive, but I wasn't comfortable driving your giant Cadillac, so I paid for all the gas. I made a really nice plate of enchiladas too."

"Money doesn't make up for it," she said. "And everyone brought nice food." We crossed the creek on a rickety bridge. Because of the big snow year, the water swelled up between the planks, splashing at our boots. The forest smelled like wet earth with a hint of woodsmoke from the surrounding houses. On the other side of the creek, new aspen leaves began sprouting, green and shiny, and a robin hopped around in the dried pine needles below.

"You were mean," she said. "You ruined the trip for me."

I apologized for being mean, for saying she hadn't been a teacher when she in fact had. I said, "I was super uncomfortable all weekend too. You know, you complain your boyfriend is passive-aggressive, but that's how you acted all weekend. Passive-aggressive."

"I wasn't about to bring it up and confront you in front of all the other girls."

"Well, you should have handled it directly, or you should have waited until later. Instead, you made passive-aggressive digs at me. That's a way of being mean too."

She admitted this was probably true. We followed the wide fire road downhill, walking side by side but both looking ahead. Then she said, "You have to decide if you want to continue our friendship. Are you going to let politics ruin our twenty-year friendship?"

I wanted to say I had enough friends, to tell her it would be easier to go our separate ways. I wanted to say this wasn't about politics but about ethics and ideology and opposite worldviews, but I stayed silent because I wasn't sure if I was ready to end the friendship. And I remembered what my mother had told me: "Don't let him win. Tell me what you're about to throw away?"

Years earlier we had been skiing at Mammoth during another storm day. I followed Brenda to the top of a cornice, and we fought the wind. Brenda dropped off into the expanse of white, but when I looked over the edge, all I could see was a foggy net, obscuring the steep slope below. I was on my telemark skis and felt less stable than I would have on my alpine equipment. Vertigo seemed to tug at me, and I couldn't move. I stood at the ridgeline as the wind buffeted against me. I waited for many minutes until another skier came to the edge and I could follow him over the cornice, keep my eyes on him instead of the dizzying white void. When I finally reached the lift, Brenda was waiting for me. She screamed at me, her voice shaking: "Don't you ever do that to me again. You scared me."

I started to cry.

We loaded the lift together, and I told her I froze there and there was nothing I could do until I could follow another skier over the cornice, and she said, "I'm sorry. Just never do that to me again."

I nodded. We sat on the chairlift in silence, and I told myself she had yelled at me because she was worried because she cared about me, and I tried to let it go.

Brenda and I followed the hiking trail for a while in silence and then crossed the creek again on a bigger wooden bridge that smelled of creosote. I said, "I need to feel like I understand where my friends are coming from. Just tell me what you like about the president. I don't understand."

She rattled off the sound bites. *Make America Great Again. Drain the Swamp. Crooked Hillary.* When she got to "I *do* think we need to build a wall," I said many immigrants are fleeing dangerous situations. And now children are being separated from their parents. Even babies are put into cages.

"If they come into this country illegally, that's the risk they take. It's their own fault. They should know better." Bright-red snow plants emerged from the soil like tiny red explosions.

"People are in real danger." I tried to steady my shaking voice. "Not all of them."

Then I asked about the pussy grabbing, the racist language, the tweets. We navigated the loose pebbles on the trail, the erosion from above-average snowfall.

"I don't like the tweets. I want to cut off his thumbs," she said, then added some version of this: "Boys will be boys; it's just locker-room talk. And I don't think he's a racist."

We walked on. I'm sure I was shaking my head. What more could I say?

I remembered asking my friend Kate how she handled similar conversations with some of her family, and she had said, "There's no room for dialogue. Everyone is too entrenched."

Brenda said, "Don't you care about your retirement? I care about money."

"I care more about people than I care about money," I said.

"I won't talk anymore politics with you. I'm done talking about it," she said. And there it was. Brenda always told me you shouldn't ask someone something if you can't take the answer. I received the answers I somehow knew I would get, and I wasn't sure I could handle them, but I could not leave the questions unasked; that pretense felt worse.

We joined the main trail back toward my house. Wildflowers were starting to bloom: mountain phlox, lupine, and mule's ears. The air smelled like sage and springtime. I said some version of this: "I can't be my true self if I can't express my beliefs. I need to be able to be my true self with my friends."

"I told you. I won't talk politics with you."

We were at an impasse; I knew that. Kate had been right: there was no space for any kind of meaningful exchange. But could I have a friendship without it? I didn't know.

Because there wasn't much more to say, we hiked on in silence. Stray patches of snow lingered in the shade. Wet pine needles crunched beneath our boots. Steller's jays squawked to each other from the lodgepoles and Jeffrey pines above.

We reached my driveway, and Brenda said, "So, do you want to continue with this friendship or not? You decide."

Was this a mountain I was willing to die on? I still wasn't sure. I wondered why it was on me, why it was my decision. I also wonder now why I didn't ask her. Maybe it's also true that I have always been a little afraid of Brenda, so I always backed away when I saw our friendship entering the danger zone. It wasn't so much that we didn't agree but that we weren't allowed to give voice to our opinions in front of each other, a kind of silencing.

I wanted nothing more than to say no. I wanted to wish her the best but say I couldn't invest any more time into the friendship. I wanted to say this was a mountain I would die on, the rocky place where our friendship finally perished. I stood there for a moment, feeling oddly calm, and then said, "We've been friends for a long time. Your friendship is important to me . . ."

Brenda started to cry and hugged me. She told me she was afraid I was going to say no and she would lose me. "Our friendship," she said, "is important to me too."

I nodded, and she got into her car. I watched her drive away, and then I walked inside, not sure what had just happened but knowing there would be another trigger later.

I have always had trouble letting things go, evidenced by my move back in with my ex-husband. Brenda moved back in with her ex around the same time I did. That's one of the things we had in common when we first met teaching skiing together, one of the mutualities we bonded over all those years ago. I once asked her why she thought we both kept trying longer than we should. "Are we assholes?"

She said no, it was that we were both used to working hard for what we wanted and neither of us give up easily. That this was a strength of character, not a weakness. We had both tried everything in our power to make things work.

They didn't work, of course, for either of us—things eventually went downhill, and we both left our exes for good, and maybe that was enough loss, so we clung to our friendship, despite seeing the world in such different ways.

I can't speak for Brenda, but I can say I have always been motivated by fear and guilt. I'm afraid of losing something, even if I no longer want it. And I feel badly, too, for discarding something I once wanted, believing it was easier to hold onto something you aren't sure you want than to get back something you realize you shouldn't have thrown away. Until the day she died, my mother lamented the loss of the things she had brought from England and stored because she couldn't pay the rent on the storage unit. Whenever she looked at an old photo, she pointed to the coat or the gloves and said, "Those were in that damned unit. Lost forever. Such a shame."

When she died, I would have had even more stuff to go through had she been able to afford the storage bill, but even so, I find myself looking at old photographs of the Penny Lane coat and the shearling gloves with something like yearning.

And there is this too: Brenda and I are both the daughters of alcoholic fathers. When I read the laundry list of characteristics of "adult children of alcoholics," I see myself—constantly seeking approval, fear of losing control, terrified of abandonment so I will do anything to hold on. That's what happens when your entire childhood was built on shaky ground. Sometimes there were avalanches, even when the danger seemed low, so I learned to stay vigilant. As with most alcoholic families, I grew up in a house of denial, of pretending, of skating across ice always about to shatter. Perhaps in our own ways, Brenda and I were both being careful, protecting ourselves in the ways we had learned.

Brenda moved away to Utah, but when she came back to visit, we met for hikes, bike rides, lunches. Over pho one day, she told me about a show she watched, something about women who were drugged and sold into the sex trade. "Some people don't have choices," she said. "That show changed my entire outlook."

I interpreted this as a change in her worldview. She recognized her privilege. She was telling me she had changed her mind! This was the way I could live inside the friendship; I assumed certain things, even though I was too afraid to ask if they were true.

Extreme Avalanche Danger: Avoid all avalanche terrain.

We are on the precipice of a pandemic. Brenda is teaching ski-ing in Utah, and she tells me the mountain might shut down. This is in the early days, when something like this—a ski resort closing—is impossible to fathom.

Days earlier the president called the coronavirus a hoax at a campaign rally and said at a news briefing that the virus was going to go away, disappear like some sort of miracle—he had "a hunch."

I am on my way to the annual women's Mammoth ski trip. I am at a gas station on Highway 395, and while I'm waiting for my gas to pump, Brenda and I exchange texts. I tell her I'm scared because no one can get tested and we are going through this with such poor leadership.

She writes back, stating that she "strongly disagrees" with my comment about the leadership in this country.

I see I was wrong; she hasn't changed her mind, but still I text her back, saying it's hard for me to believe she disagrees (because it is), and she sends me this text: *Do you really want to continue on this path with me and put our friendship in jeopardy again? I will no longer comment on your political pokes at me. Please don't put our political differences ahead of our friendship.*

I do not respond. Or rather, I write a very long text that night about how the president had called the virus a hoax and how this really will come to a life-or-death situation for many Americans.

And then I delete it.

I ask my friend Jen if she's friends with any of the MAGA crowd. She says she isn't. We live in liberal California, after all, where we have surrounded ourselves with more of ourselves and knowing a supporter is akin to finding a unicorn but without the hearts and rainbows.

"But," Jen says, "I do have a friend who is a Christian, and she thinks I'm going straight to hell. That's sort of the same thing, isn't it?"

I'm not exactly sure *how* it's the same thing but agree it somehow *feels* the same—a difference not just of opinion but of an entire worldview, but maybe more than that; with both situations it's a closed case, and there's nothing more anyone can say.

After the pandemic shuts down all the ski resorts across the country, I have been skiing the backcountry more, even though I'm not sure I should take these sorts of risks. I'm conservative, always choosing a low-angle route, but as I've learned, safety is nothing more than a superstition. I justify my decisions, the way we all do.

Climbing mountains has given me the time to think, and I keep going back to my last text interaction with Brenda, which is now more than six weeks ago. Despite the long history, maybe there has always been too much instability beneath, like a weak layer deep in the snowpack, undetectable until the moment the avalanche crown breaks loose and the slab releases, becoming a white, destructive channel of snow.

Because it's spring and we have had no new snow for a while, the avalanche danger has been low but only in the mornings, when the snowpack is still solid from the overnight freeze. As the sun climbs the sky, the hazards increase. The hope is to time our outings so we are skiing a few inches of melt-freeze, a slushy layer we call "corn snow" that's fun to ski but not yet dangerous. Once the snowpack melts and becomes wet through, what was safe in the morning becomes a considerable danger in the afternoon. As with so many things, timing is everything, and maybe that's true of friendships too. Perhaps certain friendships match certain times in our lives, but later on, what once worked no longer does. Even though it goes against my nature, I have learned to give up on things that are too difficult, to let go of people who no longer make sense, to call it a day and get off the mountain if things enter the danger zone.

Brenda still matters to me, so I come home after a day of backcountry skiing, and I finally text her back; I'm afraid she will say something about the many weeks that have passed without a response. I start a new conversation, something that has nothing to do with our previous exchange, and the conversation picks up right where it left off, or at least it seems to. After some back and forth, I tell her about my new book, *Bad Tourist*, coming out, and she writes, *Your new book sounds great! When and where can I buy it?*

She means what she says, so I know she isn't pretending to be nice, though it's clear we are both pretending in other ways. But when she says she's happy for me, I know it's true. Everything always changes, yet some things stay the same.

Or at least they seem to.

A few weeks later a mutual friend tells me Brenda has moved back to town. I tell my friend she must be mistaken.

I text Brenda and ask her, and she confirms what my friend has told me.

I am the one who is mistaken.

Brenda's texts are cryptic—I ask questions, but all I get is a yes or no. When I ask if her boyfriend has moved back with her, she says no but doesn't explain. I tell her I've been riding my bike a lot. She says she's adopted a dog. I send the last text, saying I'm here if she wants to chat.

That's the last text bubble in our exchange.

I can tell myself we are all on COVID lockdown—that's why she isn't reaching out. But I know this isn't true—the terrain, it seems, has proven too dangerous, and as it turns out, this is a mountain our friendship will die on. That white space after my text reminds me of the loss, and I tell myself it's okay to both let go and grieve.

I finally write to Brenda a month later, a response to my own text since she hasn't written back. I acknowledge the separation, telling her I understand. I wish her well. I write it as the sun is setting over the mountains. Something about that makes this feel like I'm doing the right thing at the right time. I tell her she's been a better friend to me than most. I thank her. I tell her I understand we have grown apart. This is my way of saying goodbye.

I do not hear from her for another month. I am mountain biking with Christine, and I feel my phone buzz in my pocket. Something in me knows it's her.

She says she hopes I'm having a good summer. She says she wants me to drop off the backcountry ski poles I borrowed. She acknowledges what I have written with two words: "nice note."

Later I show my husband. I ask him if he thinks this is her way of creating closure, asking for ski poles in June. I wonder if she's extending an olive branch. My husband tells me to take the message only for what it is—return the ski poles—so I do.

The most difficult avalanche to predict is the glide avalanche, which begins with a crack, where the snow breaks free from the rest. And at some point the slab breaks, taking all the snow layers with it, leaving the snow-scraped earth and a massive tree-snapping path of destruction. Sometimes the glide crack is there for months before the avalanche; other times the crack emerges seconds before the slide, giving no warning at all before the snow lets loose, destroying everything in its path.

Words Etched into Skin

My mother was the president of my fan club, and truth be told, she was also the vice president and secretary. She worked at Orchard Supply Hardware, and whenever I published a book, she brought copies to work and guilted people who would never read poetry otherwise into buying my slim volumes of verse. She also had a trick in which she would bring my memoir everywhere she went and open it as if she were reading it, or maybe she really was rereading it, in the hopes that someone would ask her about the book in her hands. "I sell a lot of books that way," she said. "My accountant hiked the John Muir Trail too. I got him to buy *Almost Somewhere.*" In truth she talked him into a very small discount off her tax preparation in a trade.

This was all very cute and sweet until my husband gave my mother his old iPhone. I was shocked at how quickly she took it up, scrolling through Facebook, shouting to me in the next room: "That distinguished gentleman in India liked my post again!" Mother's affinity for the internet meant she could google me and my writing anytime she wanted to. The days when I could publish poems in obscure literary journals she would only read if I gave them to her were gone.

One of my subjects was about how I was afraid of becoming my mother.

Like many women, my relationship with my mother was difficult. I do not have children, so it's hard for me to understand the feeling that another person is still part of my body, but that's how my mother felt. At least that's how it seemed to me. If I stubbed my toe, she would bend over as if she could feel the pain, and maybe she really did feel it. There was no such thing as a boundary in our relationship. This also meant my mother could love me and hate me in the same ways she loved and hated herself, which were complicated and varied. She was a survivor in every sense of the word, but still she carried the things she survived, and these are the things she brought to mothering me.

When I went through puberty and started dating boys, Mother called me a slut. I didn't understand that really, she had been ashamed of herself for going with married men, for using them for holidays, dresses, money. For being, in her own words, a "good-time girl." I knew she loved me, but without a boundary between us, she called me all the things she believed about herself.

I didn't realize any of this, though—not until much later, after she was gone.

Before my father died, he told me this: "Please don't break up with your mother." He saw how our lack of boundaries might be the end of us. I had always thought he said this for me. But when my mother was diagnosed with terminal cancer and I left my job and my husband to move in with her to take care of her, I realized he had said it to protect not me but her. He worried that after he was gone, there would be no one left to keep the peace.

That would be left up to me.

While Mother was dying, I wrote my way through it in order to "keep the peace." That, and I walked and I cried, but only when Mother wasn't around since I wasn't allowed to cry in front of her. She said, "You can cry on your own time." The only moments I had away from her when she was sick were on my walks with my dog, so that's when I cried, at times howling like an injured animal, upsetting my dog and scaring the neighbors. Or I cried during the short breaks between chemotherapy, when I drove the eight hours home to visit my husband and to ski.

During this time a friend asked me about the writing I was working on. We were riding up the gondola in Mammoth, so I didn't have much time to go into it. We would soon arrive at the top. I said, "I'm working on a book about how I don't want to become my mother."

"That's terrible," she said. "You should respect your mother."

I felt first the flash of anger and then the guilt. She didn't know my mother. How could she know how I felt? I loved my mother, but I didn't want to become her. Why couldn't I tell the truth about that? My friend was born in another country, so I wrote it off as a cultural difference, got off the gondola, and skied down. Though I never forgot how I felt—not just guilty but silenced.

I think about this exchange now that my mother is gone. Not because I believe I should have respected my mother more but because I couldn't have known what I now know: there are more ways I want to be like my mother than I could have believed when she was alive. There is no way, through all my imagining and my fear, I could have seen through to what is clear now.

When my mother was sick, I tried to see my future self without her, and I would say things I thought I should say: "You have been a good mother."

She would respond with something like this: "Too bad I don't have a better daughter."

And then I would cry, and she would remind me not to cry in front of her. Or she would say she was joking, and I would tell her it wasn't a very funny joke. And she would say, "What's happened to your sense of humor, girl?"

I realized I could not speak from my future self. I could only live there in the difficult moments with her. And the truth was, in some ways she wasn't a good mother.

That was a hard sentence to write, and I want to delete it, because I can hear my mother's voice asking: *How could you say such a thing about me?*

The truth was she did the best she could, which was true of me too.

My mother could not tell me I was a good daughter. She knew she was dying, and there is something in this admission— maybe what she was leaving behind—that would have destroyed her.

I'd meant to write about writing here. And about how to do that without the president of my fan club.

I will try again.

I tell my creative writing students to draft without thinking about an audience. I do that. But when I published things, I couldn't help but think about my audience, my mother.

I wrote a weird little lyrical essay called "The Essay Determines How It Will Begin" that was published in an online journal. It was about my mother and the ways her life and upbringing influenced me and my life and, ultimately, my writing. I was worried about what she would think when she found it on her new iPhone, so I called her.

When she answered the phone, she did not say hello. She said, "I already saw it."

There was no need to ask, "Saw what?" We both knew why I was calling. And I was tired of pretending. So I asked, "What did you think?"

"Well, you're a good writer." Then after a few seconds of silence, she added, "You can really make things up."

Now I was silent, unsure what she meant.

"Well, you made all of that up. This is fiction," she continued.

"Mom, I didn't make anything up. Everything's true."

"You were never locked in a coal room with the spiders."

"Mom, that was about you."

She went silent again, as she often did when I said something she didn't want to hear. Then she changed the subject, and the discussion was over. I felt an incredible sense of relief. We had come to an agreement. She could let go of the painful memories of her past because I was writing them down. And later she would leave me her journals and her letters, where she told all her stories, some I had heard and others I hadn't. The president of my fan club wanted me to tell it all.

When I could no longer deny Mother was dying, I let her read my book manuscript, the one that was about how I hoped I wasn't becoming her. She sat on the couch, the day turning to night, and she read the whole thing in one sitting. I moved about around her, bringing her food and then tea, clearing her plates. Unless you have watched someone read your work, it's hard to explain how uncomfortable this is, even if the writing isn't about the person who is reading it, and in this case it was.

When she finished, I asked her what she thought. She said, "I didn't know I had such an influence on you."

"Well, you did," I said.

"And I don't think you are the way you are because of me," she said. "And if you inherit things like the way I worry, that's good. It makes you smart."

I took notes, writing down the things she said.

"But I don't like some of it," she went on. "Some of it I don't like at all."

I kept writing, hoping she would tell me which parts she didn't like. By then her hair had fallen out, and what she had left was stretched into a little bun at the back of her head. Her scalp shined through the strands of dyed brown hair. I had written about her and about us. I had told stories from her childhood, the ones that formed who she was to become. But she didn't say a word about those stories. Instead, she said, "You and all those men. You could have gotten a disease, you know?"

No matter how many mean things my mother has said to me, I cannot deny that she was the president of my fan club. Or maybe she was my entire fan club, though that's not entirely true either. This morning a very young woman wrote to me, saying she loved one of my books so much that she wants to tattoo a line from it onto her body. She wondered if I would write it for her, so the tattoo artist might sketch it into her skin in my handwriting.

My mother's voice came into my mind: *Tell her no.*

My friend Ilyse once said when we let the words into the world, they no longer belong to us. That's what I told the young woman. That and to wait a few years, which is probably something my mother would say.

The last thing I said to Mother was "I forgive you. Please forgive me."

Or at least that's the last thing I heard myself say to her. The last thing I really said to her was this: "I'll be back in an hour. I'm going running."

The last thing she said to me was "I know you are."

The last thing she really said, according to the hospice nurse, was my name.

After she died, I wondered if letting her read the book manuscript had been cruel. But as time has gone by, I realize my former self, the one who still had a mother, made the decision that felt right to her at the time, and the self I am now should probably stay out of it. I also realize this: the president of your fan club should be trusted to read it all.

Mother Keeps Daddy on the Shelf

I.

Mother places Daddy on the bookshelf between Dante and Shirley MacLaine. I go to my old room, where Mother keeps teddy bears, Dr. Seuss, Barbie's Dreamhouse—for your children, she says. I am twenty-four, and I lie on the narrow bed, stare at the sea-foam ceiling, try to ignore my beating heart.

Later Mother asks me if I want him. I imagine breaking the seal of the smooth wooden urn. The wind scissoring through the seagrass; the air tasting like brine; the echo of memory like the wheels of my girlhood wagon over the wooden planks of the Fire Island boardwalk.

When I was little, we had a small house in Fair Harbor, and Daddy taught us how to swim and dig for clams there. It was the place he would collaborate with other writers from New York City. Where—for a few sunlit moments—he could dip into the ocean and escape the black hole of his depression.

I imagine sifting through the fragments of gray bone, offering him to the sky, watching him float over the Fire Island dunes, settling among the driftwood, shells, and beach glass. Released to the eastern sky and the Atlantic Ocean.

Mother said no, absolutely not. "You aren't taking him anywhere. He's just fine here with me."

2.

When I come back to visit Mother, I look for Daddy, but he's no longer on the shelf. "Hey, Mom," I shout to her through the walls of her townhouse, "where's Daddy?"

She walks into the den, ignores my question, is humming the melody from "The Music of the Night," occasionally singing the few words she knows.

"What have you done with Daddy?"

Mother walks past me and to the cupboard, opens it, and says, "He's right here. He's fine."

"What's this?" I ask, pointing to a Filofax on top of Daddy's urn.

"Oh, those are divorce papers from all of his ex-wives."

"You mean both?"

"That's right." Mother sings, "La dee da doo," her mouth like a peony, opening and closing.

3.

Later I sneak into the den to steal Daddy. Not all of him. Just some. Daddy, I decide, has done enough time on shelves and in filing cabinets.

I open the box, scoop out a few spoonfuls of ash into a ziplock baggie, and stuff it into my suitcase. At airport security I wonder if anyone will see the bone fragment and ask me what it is, but they don't.

I bring the baggie of ash to Mammoth Mountain. When I announced at age six that I wanted to learn how to ski, it had been Daddy who brought me to Mammoth. Now, all these years later, he is tucked into the pocket of my ski jacket. All day I feel invincible.

At the end of the day I stand in the afternoon light atop the cliff's edge, looking out at the Minarets. Three of my girlfriends look on. I take out the baggie and wait for a gust of wind. I shake the baggie into it, watching the ash swirl over the edge. My throat tightens, and my eyes water beneath my goggles, which takes me by surprise. Christine and Jen lean on their ski poles. After a few seconds Brenda says, "Say a few words?"

But I can't, so I shake my head and smile. I wave my ski pole to my friends, as if to say, "Let's go," and we drop into the chute. We cut fast turns in the wind-buffed snow behind me.

When I return home from Mammoth, I call my mother and say, "You know, I stole some of Daddy."

"I know you did."

"Do you care?"

"No, but he wanted to be spread under the rosebush."

"So why don't you put him there?"

"It's cold out there at night. Besides, if I have to have my fence redone, they'll dig him up."

I think about this, and it seems like she has a point.

"I took him out of the closet, and he's back on the shelf," she says. "I told you. He's fine where he is."

"What about spreading Daddy's ashes at Fire Island?" I ask again. "With Cathy and Cindy. The four of us. He would like that."

"I thought you already threw away your part on top of a mountain."

"I didn't throw it away, and it was just a tiny bit."

"Fire Island's not the same as it was. It's all mansions there now," she says.

"Everything changes, but Fair Harbor still has some of the original houses. Wouldn't you like to see it again?"

"We'll see," Mother says.

4.

My parents had always wanted to travel to Hawaii together. When they planned to go, Daddy was too sick, so soon after he died, Mother and I went together.

Many years later we are planning another mother-daughter Hawaii trip, but the week before we are to leave, Mother ends up in the hospital with lung cancer. She says, "Go with your husband."

After she dies, Tom and I leave for Kauai, and I bring my parents—not the big bags of ash, just enough.

On our way to release them at the edge of the cliff on the Maha'ulepu Heritage Trail, we pass a rooster with a crushed foot and a woman who is chemo-bald. Newlyweds pose on the rocks below, taking wedding photographs. As the wind takes the bone fragment, the light reflects silver on the ocean and two white-tailed tropic birds soar above.

It is all there: suffering and beauty, love and death, endings and the flight of new beginnings.

5.

My sisters and I book the trip to Fire Island. I pull the big bags of bone fragment out of their respective urns—a cedar box for Daddy that the lady at the mortuary shamed us into buying and a broken plastic box for mother—the cheapest option, which is what she would have wanted.

I put Daddy in first. When I try to place Mother into the suitcase, ash spills out all over the bottom of my case. I pull the bag out, and even though I have double-bagged her, ash scatters everywhere. By the time I hurry the bag into a third jumbo freezer bag, my suitcase, bedroom floor, and clothes are covered in ash. "Mother!" I say, "I know you're doing this on purpose. But I don't care what you say. You're going to Fire Island." I shove her in next to Daddy, who is sitting at the bottom of my suitcase, neatly behaved.

Before she dies, Mother says, "If I pop off, you can keep me and Daddy in your closet."

"No way," I say. "You're going in the ocean. Or coming with me to Burning Man."

"No water," she says. "And you better not take me to the desert either. Maybe I can go on top of that mountain with Riva, so I can look over you?" But then she says, "But that would be too cold in the winter, wouldn't it? The closet is better."

As it turns out, I take both parents to Hawaii and Burning Man. I let a bit of her go on top of Mount Tallac and in the same place as Daddy at the top of chair 23 in Mammoth too. And every time, my father's ashes float away. But when it comes to Mother, the wind picks up or shifts every time, coating me with her ash. In this way we continue our arguments long after she's gone—and she always gets the last word.

I set my clothes on top of my parents, zip up my suitcase, and say, "Off to Fire Island."

At airport security my luggage is pulled from the conveyor. The agent points to my suitcase and says, "Is this yours?" I nod and follow him. He brings up the picture on the screen and points at the two plastic bags of ash. He tells me he is going to open my bag, and I nod again. He unzips my suitcase, pushes aside my clothes and toiletries, and there they are. "What is this?" he asks, but it seems like he already knows.

"Those . . . are my parents."

He looks me in the eye, and he says, "I'm supposed to go through these."

I start to cry, which surprises me, though I have learned that the waves of grief can come anytime. And then I hear Mother saying, *Well, if I've got to be fondled, at least he's cute.* Now I'm standing there with tears on my face, trying not to laugh. This, more than anything, defines those who are grieving: crying but trying not to laugh. Laughing and trying not to cry. Always, always feeling everything alongside its opposite.

He pushes my clothes back over my parents, closes the lid of my suitcase, and says in a very quiet voice, "But I'm not going to. I'm sorry for your loss."

I zip my suitcase, pull it onto the ground, thank him, and roll my bag toward the terminal.

When I tell Cathy and Cindy my mother's ash spilled all over, that I was stopped at security, they say, "That's *so* Sheila," meaning my mother. They have known her since our father married her when they were fourteen and seventeen.

We decide to spread the ashes at dawn, when the beach is empty. I carry both bags in my backpack, and they feel heavy, but something about that feels right too. We walk along the beach until the first rays of sunlight appear on the watery horizon. It's time. We walk to the water's edge. I unzip my pack and hand over Daddy to my sisters. I pull out Mother.

We look at each other, open our bags, which takes me longer because now Mother is triple bagged, and we dump the ash into the water. There is no wind, carrying them away, as I had imagined. There is only a cloudy swirl in the dark-blue ocean and gray specks in the white sea-foam. I can hear Mother say, *No water!* But I know this isn't for her. This is for me and my sisters. We needed to let Daddy go there, and wouldn't she be angrier if we hadn't brought her along?

I pull my empty backpack over my shoulders. My sisters and I walk along the beach for a long time in silence; dawn flickers into day, and our shadows stretch across the wet sand before us.

And because Mother always gets her way, I had held back a thimble of her ash and stored it in my jewelry box, among the rings and pins she left me. She's tucked away safely in my closet, where she always wanted to be.

Ways to Speak the Unspeakable

1. Think in shards. It's already broken, so you'll be telling the truth.

2. State the obvious. "You still have your tree up," you say. It's the middle of June. A Star of David perches at the top of the artificial Christmas tree. "We never take it down," she says, "why bother now?"

3. Don't state the obvious. She says she can't write a memoir: "How can I? I don't know the arc." You say, "Just write." "But the arc," she says. "I don't know how it will end." What hair she has left is stretched into a bun, the shine of skull between strands.

4. Figure out who's to blame. Her childhood home was near the largest repository of nuclear weapons in the world. "At least there's a reason," she says. "Twenty-five hundred warheads. This isn't my fault." Never say there's no one to blame.

5. Get metaphysical. Toxic red algae bloomed in the gulf, killing the oysters. Believe her when she says, "I could feel it, those oysters dying. Something about the brain radiation." She can't eat oysters anymore.

6. Say ridiculous things. Ask if she's met anyone nice during chemo. As if it's a cocktail party. "It's not like that," she says. Later you'll see for yourself.

7. Rely on symbolism. Pink ribbons say everything's going to be okay. Agree on red knots, messy and hard.

8. Go meta. She asks if you mind her writing a poem about your conversations. You don't mind. You ask her if you can write something too. She agrees, says you are each other's story. After she dies, you write story after story.

9. Conjure her in your dreams. In dreamscape you ask her for the bowling ball, but she says you need a tent instead. "Trust me," she says. Before you can speak, she disappears, her hands vanishing last.

10. Say nothing at all.

Dreaming in the Time of Wildfire

Green: Good. 0 to 50. Air quality is satisfactory, and air pollution poses little or no risk.

You are in what looks like a war-torn building, with burned blackened walls and the sky lurching through holes in the roof. You climb to the top floor, looking for your mother. You call out the same refrain you shouted when you found her dead, "Mom, Mom, Mom!" You hear her laugh. It is weak, more a tittering. She is a corpse on a bed, the wind and rain and dark night coming in sideways. You go to hug her emaciated body, and she says, "Stop doing this to me." Before you can ask what she means, she says, "I won't come to you anymore. You must stop this."

The next day you tell your husband your dream, and he asks what you think it means. You tell him you have to let her go. "So let her go," he says. You laugh, the same kind of titter from your dream. Then you look at him and say, "I don't know how."

Yellow: Moderate. 51 to 100. Air quality is acceptable. However, there may be a risk for some people, particularly those who are unusually sensitive to air pollution.

You are back at work in Tahoe, staying in the dorms with your graduate students. You wake early to a white sky, a pinprick pink sun burning through. A new fire, the Caldor, 752 acres.

Underneath the pall of smoke, the students are masked, lining up for COVID tests. You join them for your nose swab.

Your husband is in Canada and leaving for a canoe trip that afternoon, and you won't hear from him for ten days, not even a text. You tell him a new fire has started and you're worried. He says, "Yes, there's a lot of fuel to burn." By fuel he means forest, and you cannot stop the tears.

Later you learn the fire has reached areas affected by the large blowdown event last winter. This is often described as interacting forest disturbances, resulting in unexpected fire behavior.

Orange: Unhealthy for Sensitive Groups. 101 to 150. Members of sensitive groups may experience health effects. The general public is less likely to be affected.

You dream your dorm room is burning. You wake up, choking on the smoke, think, "It really is on fire." You run to switch on the light. You close your window, grab your phone to look up the air quality index. It isn't a fire inside, you tell yourself. It is the world outside that's burning.

Steep drainages and canyons in the region have continued to aid erratic winds and hamper control efforts. The fire has grown to 22,919 acres. Containment is at 0 percent.

Red: Unhealthy. 151 to 200. Some members of the general public may experience health effects; members of sensitive groups may experience more serious health effects.

Despite the smoke, your students still want to hold class outdoors so they don't have to wear their masks. Your eyes are stinging and your lungs are aching, but you agree.

During class a bewildered bear cub wanders by. You tell your students to ignore it. "But what about the mama?" one of the student asks. You can tell there is no mama, know there's nothing to be done, and don't want to reveal the sad facts to your students. 43,858 acres.

After class you scroll through the reports, a new lexicon of fire: *candling, creeping, spotting, torching, extreme fire behavior.*

Purple: Very Unhealthy. 201 to 300. Health alert: the risk of health effects is increased for everyone.

Your house is in the path of the fire. But here at the college you are on the other side of the lake. Even though there is no immediate danger where you are, some of your colleagues flee the smoke. One by one they board airplanes. The students cannot afford to do the same. In extreme fire conditions, predictability is difficult because such fires often exercise some degree of influence on their environments and behave erratically, sometimes dangerously.

You finish your teaching duties, head back to your house to rescue things. But what things? What would your husband want? You walk around the house, wondering what you can live without. Everything. Nothing. You call your sister-in-law, wander room to room, distracted. You ask her what your husband might want. She says, "Just take what matters to you and go."

You pull some art from the walls, a few of your husband's favorite flannels, a Moroccan rug you paid too much for in Marrakech.

Before leaving, you water your plants. "It's not your fault," you tell them. "You shouldn't have to suffer too."

You thank your house and then walk out into the raining ash, the brown sky. You drive north, nearly throw up on yourself in the car, sick from the smoke.

Highway 50, the road into your hometown, is closed both ways. 104,309 acres.

Maroon: Hazardous. 301 and higher. Health warning of emergency conditions: everyone is more likely to be affected.

You do not know how this story will end, so you flee now at 149,684 acres, before the evacuation orders come. Head to the coast, breathe in the clean foggy air, walk along the beach with your friend Nancy. Her phone buzzes. She glances down at it and says, "Oh no. Uncle Wes has died of COVID."

"I'm so sorry," you say. "We're living in Crisisland." Nancy nods.

You walk on together, avoiding the purplish jellyfish that have washed onto shore. You breathe in the sweet rot at the ocean's edge, watch the lacy foam bubble on the sand and disappear.

But then you spot a rafter of wild turkeys under the eucalyptus trees. You both stop to watch them, listen to their strange and soft cooing. For a moment there is no fire and no pandemic, just the brown striated miracle of these large birds.

You dream you are at a party and your mother comes to the door. She is part woman, part old dog, and she leans up against you because she is too weak to stand. You help her in, seat her in a recliner next to your friend Andy, who is eating popcorn from a blue ceramic bowl.

You say to your mother, "I thought you weren't going to come back to me. That I wouldn't see you again." She looks up at you from her lounge chair and says, "I know. I wasn't going to, but I'm addicted." Before you can ask what she means, even though you already know, she turns into a pile of kindling.

You reach for a piece of her and wake up, your hair still smelling of smoke.

Acknowledgments

I am grateful to Rob Taylor and the University of Nebraska Press for believing in my work once again. Many thanks to Brian Turner for granting me permission to use part of Ilyse Kusnetz's poem "Holding Albert Einstein's Hand" from *Small Hours* (Alice James Books, 2014). I also wish to thank the editors of the following publications and websites, where some of these essays first appeared, sometimes in slightly different forms or with different titles:

The Bark: "The Last Goodbye"

Brevity: "Bone & Skin"; "The Essay Determines How It Will Begin"

CNN: "A Love Letter to My Hometown after the Shooting"

Creative Nonfiction: "The Grief Scale"; "The Same Story"

Hunger Mountain Review: "In Love with the World"

The Kiss: Intimacies from Writers: "A Kiss for the Dying"

The Manifest Station: "Friending the Dead"

Mead Magazine: "The Hungry Bride"

The Midnight Oil: "The Red Canoe"

New York Times: "Wearing Her Eye Shadow"

River Teeth: "Becoming Bird"

The Rumpus: "Breaking the Codes"

Santa Fe Writers Project: "Honky-Tonk Woman"

Southern Sin: True Stories of the Sultry South and Women Behaving Badly: "Sportfucking"

Tahoe Blues: Short Lit on Life at the Lake: "Eight Hours"

Wanderlust Journal: "Traveling Alone"; "Traveling with the Dead"; "Winter Travel"